Tibet struggle, a China minority Environment
History, Custom and Tradition

Author
Steven Willis

Copyright Notice

Copyright © 2017 Global Print Digital
All Rights Reserved

<u>Digital Management Copyright Notice</u>. This Title is not in public domain, it is copyrighted to the original author, and being published by **Global Print Digital**. No other means of reproducing this title is accepted, and none of its content is editable, neither right to commercialize it is accepted, except with the consent of the author or authorized distributor. You must purchase this Title from a vendor who's right is given to sell it, other sources of purchase are not accepted, and accountable for an action against. We are happy that you understood, and being guided by these terms as you proceed. Thank you

First Printing: 2017.

ISBN: 978-1-912483-58-7

Publisher: Global Print Digital.
Arlington Row, Bibury, Cirencester GL7 5ND
Gloucester
United Kingdom.
Website: www.homeworkoffer.com

.

Table of Content

Introduction 1
History 3
   Tibet Rulers 7
      Princess Wencheng A famous queen in Tibetan history 8
      Songtsen Gampo Tibetan King 10
      Story of Songtsan Gambo and Princess Wencheng 12
      Tubo Kingdom in Tibet's History 16
      Powerful Guge Kingdom in Tibetan History 18
      Influential Figures in Tibet History 20
Geography and Environment 24
   The Elevation Change in 7 Major Regions of Tibet 25
   Agriculture and Climate in Tibet 32
   Environment of Tibet 37
Tibet Local Customs 43
   Tibetan Funerals & Relevant Taboos 44
   The Sporty Side of Tibet 49
   Sky Burial in Tibet and Tibetan Funeral Customs 56
   Tibetan Tea Culture at The Roof of The World 62
   Tibetan Marriage Customs, Wedding Ceremony in Tibet 64
   Tibetan Etiquettes 68
   Mystical Tibetan Funeral Practices 73
   Mani Stones in Tibet 76
   Qiema Box - Essential Mascot for Tibetan New Year 79
   Tibet Traditional Wedding 80
   hatag, an Auspicious Symbol in Tibetan Culture 82
   Don'ts in Tibet 84
   Wooden Bowls Play a Key Role in Tibetan Culture 86
   Yak Racing, a Spectator Sport in Tibet 89
   Witness to a Sky Burial in Tibet 90
   Sweet Tea, Tibetan People's Coffee 94
   Replacing Valance on Tibetan New Year's Eve 96
   Weisang, Tibetan Households' Custom 97
   Gutu, Tibetan New Year Reunion Dinner 100

- Why Tibetan People Worship Yak Head 101
- Tibetan Adult Ceremony for Girls 103
- Tibetan Birth Ceremony 105
- Ritual Walk Season in Tibet – Saga Dawa Festival 107
- History of Prayer Flags in Tibet 109

Tibetan Culture Heritage 111
- Understanding the importance of Tibetan music 111
  - Tibetan Opera 116
  - Tibetan Heroic Epic - King Gesar 119
  - Plots of King Gesar - Tibetan Epic 123
  - Guozhuang Dance - Tibetan Dance 124
  - Zhuoxie Dance 126
  - Large-Scale Tibetan Natural Lyrics : Happiness on the Way .. 128
  - Duixie Dance - Tibetan Tap Dance 129

Tibetan Arts 131
- Tibetan Thangka Paintings 132
- Overview of Tibetan Culture and Arts 133
- Sand Mandala in Tibet and Its Profound Philosophy 141
- Tibetan Thangka Art 146
- Qamo Dance - Tibetan Religious Dance 149
- Tibetan Stone and Rock Carvings 151
- Tibetan murals - Tibet painting art 154
- Bullboat Dancing 160
- Rutog rock paintings in western Tibet 160

Tibetan Cuisine 163
- The Most Beloved Food and Beverage in Tibet 164
- Tibetan Momo, A Kind of Exotic Dumpling in Tibet 171
- The Most Significant Tibetan Culture: Sweet Tea House in Lhasa ... 177

Tibetan People 184
- Lhoba People in Sountheast of Himalayas 187
- Uncovering the great Himalayan mystery: the Yeti 193

Tibet and China history of a Complex Relationship 200
- Is Tibet Part of China? 200

The Chinese View of Tibet Is Dialogue Possible? 220
- "Tibet Is an Inalienable Part of China" 221

"Chinese Rule Has Been Good" 226
"Interference in China's Internal Affairs Is Unacceptable" 230
Is Dialogue Possible? 232

Introduction

Tibetan civilization began near the Yarlung Zanbo River in present-day Tibet. A Tibetan kingdom was created in the sixth century AD. In the seventh century, the ruler Songtsen Gampo made Lhasa the capital of Tibet. While he ruled, the Tibetan laws, calendar, alphabet, and system of weights and measures were created. Princess Wenchen, his Chinese bride, came to Tibet in 641. She had a great effect on Tibetan culture.

Warfare and political strife weakened the Tibetan dynasty and it collapsed in 877. Tibet was conquered by the Mongolians in the thirteenth and fourteenth centuries. Later it came under Chinese control. The Qing Dynasty (1644–1911) recognized Tibet's spiritual leaders, the Dalai Lama and the Panchen Lama. A local government was set up in Tibet, with its own minister from the emperor. This system continued under the Republic of China until 1949, when the communist revolution created the People's Republic of China. The new government created the Tibetan Autonomous Region, covering all of Tibet. The political power of the lamas was taken away and given to Tibetan leaders nominated by the central government in Beijing.

History

Deciding what is ancient history and what is mysterious legend is not always an easy task. Tibet is no exception. Legend tells us that history of this high land starts with a monkey and a Raksasi, a female ogre, when the monkey was sent by Avalokiteshvara (Chenrezi) for the religious training on this high plateau. The Raksasi persuade the monkey to marry her by threatening to kill thousands of people. Having the permission of Avalokiteshvara, they married and had five offspring who are believed to be the ancestors of the local people. This legend is well known and depicted in ancient books and murals. Even the name of Tsedang, the capital city of Shannan Region, means 'the place where the monkey plays'.

However, archeological and geological discoveries lead ethnologists to believe that people living on this land are descendants of aboriginal and nomadic Qiang tribes. According to archeology, history of this land can be traced back 4,000 years. At that time, life was simple, with stone implements being used. Historical records show that not until the 7th century could the livings here be recognized as a race of people. The rising Yarlung Dynasty (Tubo Kingdom) unified this land and became an aggressive power. The first palace in Tibet, Yumbu Lakang was built for its first king, Nyatri Tsenpo. His offspring, Songtsen Gampo,

the most powerful and intelligent king of Tubo, conquered other tribes and founded the first dynasty of this land, Yarlung Dynasty (Tubo Kindom). Songtsen Gampo also made great contributions to the region's culture, economy, technology, religion, etc. by communicating with the outside world. The outstanding king of the Tubo Kingdom married two princesses of Nepal and of the Tang (618-907). The Princesses brought with them advanced technology, exotic culture, tea, silk and most important of all, peace and Buddhism.

Songtsen Gampo embraced the religion and the first transmission of Buddhism came to the snowy land. The king and the princesses built Jokhang Temple and Ramoche Temple to enshrine the holy statues of Sakyamuni. They also ordered the construction of the grand Potala Palace. The king's successors followed the religion too and in 779 King Trisong Detsen set up Samye Monastery, the first Buddhist temple on this land. The great religious teacher,

Padmasambhava was invited there and Buddhism was recognized as the state religion. The Buddhist influence spread as the expansion of the Tibetan empire continued. The indigenous Bon were not satisfied with the popularity that Buddhism held with the royal family. In 836, King Ralpachen was assassinated and Lang Darma, who believed in Bon and objected to Buddhism, was installed as King. Severe persecution against Buddhists ended the first Buddhism transmission. Lang Darma, in 842, was assassinated by a Buddhist and the collapse of the Yarlong Dynasty followed causing the decentralization of the region and a struggle for power for the next 400 years.

In 1042, Atisa was invited to the land to launch the second Buddhism transmission and Buddhism gradually revived. Gradually, Tibetan Buddhism divided itself into many sects and sub-sects, which rigorously debated with each other, vying for dominance by seeking patrons among the warring principalities. In the twelfth century, the Mongol Empire rose to power and expanded aggressively. Sakyapa, or the Stripe sect, was quite powerful among all the sects at that time. The Mongol Emperor negotiated with the abbot of Sakyapa and assisted him to become the ruler of the land. From then on, the region became an appendage of the Mongol Empire. Later, the Mongol Empire conquered the Song Dynasty (960-1279) and founded the Yuan Dynasty (1271-1368). In 1254, Kublai Khan granted supreme authority over the snowy land to the leader of Sakyapa. Sakya Pandit was appointed to become the imperial preceptor and a high official in his court. The area was thus incorporated as one of the 13 provinces of China. At the end of the Yuan Dynasty, Sakyapa declined and was replaced by the Kagyu order, whose patron offered tribute to the imperial court and was conferred with titles and administrative authority. After the Ming Dynasty (1368-1644) was established, high lamas there were summoned to the imperial court to receive titles and appointments.

In 1644, Qing Dynasty replaced Ming Dynasty. In 1652, the Fifth Dalai Lama was summoned to Beijing, and in 1653 he was conferred with the title Dalai Lama and made religious leader of local Buddhism by Emperor Shunzhi (1643 - 1661). In 1727, the central government of the Qing Dynasty sent ministers there as a representative to supervise local administration. The boundary of Tibet and Sichuan, Yunnan, and Qinghai was then official set. The Qing government promulgated *Imperially Approved Ordinance for the More Efficient Governing of Tibet* concerning many issues such as the duty of representative ministers, boundary military defense, finance, tax and the management of the temples etc in 1793. Since then, the major principles of the ordinance worked as the regulation for local regime and legislation for more than a century.

In 1911, the Qing Dynasty collapsed and the Republic of China was founded. The government of Republic of China practiced the sovereignty of the area just as the Yuan, Ming and Qing Dynasties did. The central government set Mongolia and Tibet affair office and commission to execute the administration of Tibet nationality, Mongolia nationality as well as other minorities. In 1949, the People's Republic of China was founded. The PRC government adopted the policy of peace liberation and signed with local government *the Seventeenth Point Treaty*. Later in 1959, Chinese government carried out a democratic reform of abolishing feudal serf system so that hundreds of thousands of serfs and slaves were free and no longer forced to labor.

With a steady development of the next several years, the Tibet Autonomous Region was officially set up in September, 1965. Up to now, this splendid pure land has received numerous visitors from all over the world ever since it is opened to the outside world.

Tibet Rulers

Princess Wencheng A famous queen in Tibetan history

Princess Wencheng was the most famous and beloved queen in Tibetan history, with Princess Bhrikuti for Nepal. About 1,300 years ago, this beautiful and intelligent princess of the Tang Dynasty (618-907) left the capital Chang'an (present-day Xi'an in Shanxi Province) for the Tubo Kingdom, today's Tibet, which was about 2,000 miles away in the southwest. She brought the Tibetans many of the scientific and agricultural advances of the Tang dynasty and is also credited with the introduction of Buddhism into the region. She was to join Songtsan Gambo, King of Tubo, to whom her royal father had just married. It was a famous peace-making marriage in the Tang Dynasty.

Prince Wencheng was a daughter of a courtier. This interracial matrimony helped strengthen the ties between the Tang Dynasty and the Tubo Kingdom. At that time, Emperor Taizong of the Tang dynasty needed to find a bride for King Songtsen Gampo, the new ruler of the Tubo Kingdom (Tibet), and smart and pretty Wencheng seemed an ideal match. She was conferred the title of princess and sent west. The story of Princess Wencheng and Songtsan Gambo has been cherished by the Tibetans and the rest of the Chinese people ever since.

Nowadays, the statues of Princess Wencheng and Songtsan Gambo are still in the Jokhang Monastery. Songtsan Bambo had the Ramoche Monastery built for the Buddha statues that Princess Wencheng had brought with her. The princess herself also had the Jokhang Monastery built, and in front of it she and Songtsan Gambo planted some willow trees now known as tangliu (the Tang willow). Today, the original statue of Sakyamuni believed to be brought by Princess Wencheng is still enshrined in the center of the main hall of the Jokhang Monastery.

Songtsan Gambo died in 650 when he was only thirty-four years old. Prince Wencheng passed away thirty years later. A ceremonious funeral was held for the beloved princess. Generation after generation of poets have written numerous verses to eulogize her. Her story was adapted to various theatrical forms. Two traditional observations have been devoted to her: the fifteenth day of the fourth month of each Tibetan year (the day when Princess Wencheng arrived in Tubo) and the fifteenth day of the tenth month of each Tibetan year (the birthday of Princess Wencheng). When the days come each year, the Tibetan people will turn out in their best costumes to sing and dance to commemorate her. Her statue and that of Songtsan Gambo are worshiped in the Jokhang Monastery. The chamber where they spent their first married life is still kept intact in the Potala Palace.

Songtsen Gampo Tibetan King

Songtsen Gampo, the 33rd ruler of the Tubo Regime in Tibet, is an important Tibetan King in Tibet history and is considered to be the real founder of the Tibetan Empire (known as Tubo Regime in Tibet history). His contribution to the unity of the Chinese nation and his influence in establishing lines of communication between Tibet and China are part of his great legacy.

It is said that Songtsen Gampo was born at Gyama in 617, in Maldro (a region to the northeast of modern Lhasa), the son of the Yarlung king Namri Songtsen. The book The Holder of the White Lotus says that it is believed that he was an incarnation of the Buddhist Bodhisattva Avalokiteshvara, of whom the Dalai Lama are similarly believed to be a manifestation of. He is also said to have had webbed hands and feet, a deformed face and odd skin; the early Tibetans saw him as a god and enthroned him. His identification as a cakravartin or incarnation of Avalokiteśvara began in earnest in the indigenous Buddhist literary histories of the 11th Century.

Greatly influenced by his father, Songtsen Gampo has shown the singular gift since childhood. At the age of thirteen, he acceded to the throne after his father was poisoned. He established Tubo slavery regime and moved the capital to Luosuo (today's Lhasa) after he quelled the rebellions from all parts of the region. Because of his efforts, Tibet was finally unified. By making laws, regulations and tax systems, and by fostering the development of farming and stockbreeding, Tibet prospered.

At the time he took the throne, the Tibetan people did not have a writing system and kept records by tying knots. To address this, Songtsen Gampo sent sixteen nobles including the minister Thonmi Sambhota to India to study Sanskrit and writing. They created a spoken and written language, and translated the Buddhist doctrines into this new language. This contribution helped to preserve, transmit and develop the Tibetan culture.

Songthen Gampo celebrated successes in battle expanded the Tibetan empire deep into Nepal and Tang Dynasty, and it was during these battles that he gained an appreciation of the neighbouring cultures. As a reminder of the great empire that Songtsen Gampo ruled, a large pillar still stands before the Potala palace in Lhasa, erected during his reign, on which is inscribed the agreement between the Tibetan and Chinese rulers to respect each other's borders. He studied Chinese, became skilled in the art of leadership, and most importantly, he adopted sacred codes of conduct from Buddhist scripture. Under his rule, sacred practices began to replace the shamanistic practices of the Bonpos.

This great Tibetan King's marriage to two Princesses respectively from Nepal and Tang Dynasty was widely circulated. In 639, after he married Princess Chizun of Nepal, he proposed a marriage to the Tang Dynasty. In 641, the Emperor Tang Taizong sent Princess Wencheng to marry this great Tibetan king. Both the two princesses were said to introduce Buddhism to Tibet. Princess Wencheng also brought with her a wide array of advanced cultural and technological ideas of Tang Dynasty, which further promoted the economic and cultural development in Tibet.

Unfortunately, this great Tibetan King died of an illness in 650, at the age of thirty-four. Emperor Tang Gaozong, the son of the Emperor Tang Taizong, bestowed upon him the honorary title of "The King of Xihai Jun". A stone statue of him was placed next to Zhao Ling, the Mausoleum of the Emperor Tang Taizong. This high honor commemorates the friendly relationship between the Tang and Tubo Empires. It is said that Songtsen Gampo was buried in Yumbu Lakhang in southeast Tibet.

Story of Songtsan Gambo and Princess Wencheng

The story of Tibet King Songtsan Gambo and Princess Wencheng of Tang Dynasty is well known by Tibetan people as well as Han people. If you wanna know Tibet, you must know this story at first as there are many tourist sites related with this story.

The story happened about 1300 years ago when Princess Wencheng of the Tang Dynasty (618-907) left Chang'an (Xi'an) to marry Songtsan Gambo, king of the Tubo kingdom. Their marriage was aimed to maintain amicable relations between the Tang and the Tubo.

The Tang was a powerful dynasty in Chinese history. It was the civilization center of East Asia. Neighboring nations and tribes fell under the influence of the Tang Dynasty, and earnestly sought ties with the dynasty. They either claimed allegiance to the Tang or paid tributes to the imperial court. This stimulated exchanges between the Han and other nationalities.

The same period saw Songtsan Gambo gain control of the highland area in the west. After having annexed some tiny states, he founded the Tubo Kingdom and named Loso (Lhasa) the capital city. Beginning in 634, he twice dispatched Gar Tongtsan to Chang'an, where the Tubo minister informed the Tang of Songtsan Gambo's desire for a daughter of the Tang emperor. Tang Emperor Taizong agreed to let Wencheng marry the Tubo king. Accompanied by the Tubo minister, Princess

Wencheng set out for the farway Tubo Kingdom. This segment of history was later turned into tales which remain an important part of Tibetan folklore.

Princess Wencheng brought crop and vegetable seeds to Tibet, and joined her entourage in teaching the local people how to grow crops and vegetables, grind wheat flour and make wine. Besides, Princess Wencheng brought out Buddhist pagodas, scriptures and statues of Buddha which she had brought into the Tubo area for construction of monasteries.

Goats were mobilized to carry earth to fill in a pond for the construction of the Jokhang Temple. Princess Wencheng and her husband, Songtsan Gambo, planted a willow tree in front of the monastery, which later was dubbed the Tang Willow, as the Uncle-Nephew Alliance Tablet (erected in 823 to mark the alliance between the Tang and the Tubo) was placed next to the tree. The statue of Sakyamuni enshrined in the center of the Main Hall of the Jokhang Monastery was the one Princess Wencheng brought into Tubo. In the side halls flanking the Main Hall are enshrined statues of Songtsan Gambo and Princess Wencheng. Their faces were heavily gilded by incessant worshipers of later generations.

Princess Wencheng also had the Ramoche Monastery built. She named the eight surrouding mountains the Eight Treasures, a name which is still in use today. All these paved the way for the spread of Buddhism into Tubo Kingdom.

Songtsan Gambo loved Princess Wencheng so much that he had the Potala Palace built for his talented and beautiful wife. The majestic Potala Palace, with 1000 chambers, was partially damaged by thunderbolts and wars. It twice underwent repairs and expansions in the 17th century, reaching its present size, with the 13-story main structure standing 117 meters high and covering a land area of 360000 square meters.

Frescos of the Potala Palace record historical events, including Tang Emperor Taizong asking Gar Tongtsan to perform five difficult tasks before acceding to the envoy's request for his master to marry a Tang princess, the hardships Princess Wencheng endured on way to the Tubo Kingdom, and how warmly she was greeted at Lhasa. The ruins of the Tubo period behind the Potala Palace includes a chamber for Songtsan Gambo to meditate and practice Buddhism. On the four walls of the chamber hang colored statues of Songtsan Gambo, Princess Wencheng and Gar Tongtsan.

Tubo Kingdom in Tibet's History

Tubo Kingdom witnessed the most powerful period in Tibet's history. The great Tibetan leader Songtsan Gambo brought together more than 10 separate tribes during Tang Dynasty (618-907) of China, an event commonly seen as marking the establishment of the Tubo Kingdom, making his capital in present-day Lhasa. It was the Tubo Kingdom that made today's prosperous Tibetan culture and Tibetan Buddhism.

The Tibet King Songtsan Gambo also established good relations with the Tang court and benefitted from the importation of Tang technologies (advanced for the day), and was influenced by Tang culture and politics. He twice sent ministers to the Tang Dynasty court requesting a member of the imperial family be given him in marriage and in 641 he married Princess Wencheng, a member of Emperor Taizong's family

During the Tubo Kingdom, various Chinese technologies were introduced into Tibet, such as wine-making, grinding, and paper and ink making. Sons of the Tibetan aristocracy were and ink making. Sons of the Tibetan aristocracy were sent to the Tang capital Chang'an (present-day Xi' an) to study. Literati from the Tang court went to the Tibetan capital to handle communications with the emperor. During the reign of Songtsan Gambo political, economic and cultural relations between Tang and Tubo were friendly. Laudatory titles given King Songtsan Gambo by Emperor Gaozong include Commandant-escort, Commandery Prince of the Western Sea and Com panion Prince.

This pattern of friendly relations established during the reign of Songtsan Gambo was carried on during the next two hundred years. In 710 the Tang Princess Jincheng was sent to Tibet to marry the Tubo King Tride Tsugtsen, accompanied by several tens of thousands of pieces of embroidered satin brocade, a variety of technical writings and various other useful items. Princess Jincheng later gave money to support Buddhist monks from Yutian (now in modern Xinjiang) and elsewhere on their trips to Tibet to build monasteries and translate sutras. She also requested that Chinese classical works such as The Book of Songs With Annotation by Mao Heng, The Book of Rites, Zuo Qiuming's Chronicles, and Xiao Tong's Literary Selections be sent to her from the Tang court

In 821 King Chiri Pachen of Tibet three times sent envoys to Chang'an to discuss forming an alliance with the Tang Empire. Emperor Muzong ordered his prime minister to effect the alliance in a grand ceremony held in the western suburbs of the capital. The following year high-ranking representatives of the Tang court including Liu Yuanding were dispatched to Tibet to participate in a similar ceremony marking the alliance held in the eastern suburbs of Lhasa. Representatives of the Tibetan king included his chief ministers.

This all occurred during the first and second years (822 and 823) of the Changqing reign of the Tang Dynasty, and accordingly has been called the "Changqing Alliance" by historians. The two parties agreed to "amity as though they were of one family" and to "treat their sacrificial alters as though they were one." An account of the alliance is recorded on three tablets, and the "Tang- Tubo Alliance Tablet", one of the three, still stands before the Jokhang Temple in Lhasa.

The Tubo Kingdom of the boom years Tibetans have about 15 million. Distribution is also wider, Tibet Part of the Imagawa, Yunnan, Gansu, Qinghai, and new major regions and countries and regions of Nepal, Bhutan, Sikkim, and Kashmir. But, the Tubo Kingdom began to decline since 842 and finally taken place by Guge Kingdom.

Powerful Guge Kingdom in Tibetan History

Guge Kingdom is another powerful kingdom in Tibetan history after the mighty Tubo Kingdom. From the middle 10th century to the early 17th century, Guge Kingdom governed the western Tibet, spreading

Buddhism and resisting outer attacks. Guge Kingdom played an important role in the history after the Tubo Kingdom in Tibet.

The history of Guge Kingdom can be dated back to the late Tubo Kingdom period. The royalty of Guge Kingdom was the direct descendants of Tubo Zamprogna (similar to the king in Chinese).

In the 9th century, the once-prosperous Tubo Kingdom gradually declined. The last Zamprogna Langdama (Tibet King) implemented the policy of eradicating Buddhism. As a result, contradictions between the monks group and the secular blue blood group among the rulers were intensified and wars broke out. Langdama died in a war in the year of 823. His sons and grandsons fought for the thrones. Jide Nimagun was defeated in the battles and escaped to the remote Nagri area. Later, he created a powerful kingdom-Guge Kingdom in Nagri area. In his late years, in order to avoid the tragedy of fight between brothers, he divided the Guge Kingdom into three parts and gave them respectively to his three sons.

In the beginning, the Guge Kingdom ruled that Buddhism was the foundation principle to govern the whole kingdom. The governors were all quite enlightened. They built the Tuolin Monastery and translated the Buddhism scriptures to spread Buddhism.

However, in the later Guge Kingdom period, the monks group got stronger and stronger, becoming the threat to the royalty. So the last king of Guge Kingdom decided to believe in Catholicism and built some Catholic churches. The monks group then staged an uprising. What's worse, they seduced the enemies of Guge Kingdom-Ladake to attack Guge Kingdom. As a result, the kingdom was destroyed by internal disorder and invasion from the outside.

Nowadays, the ruins of Guge Kingdom become a great tourist attraction in western Tibet. The ruins cover an area of 200,000 square meters. The buildings follow the hill to its top in a rigid layout and an imposing manner. The 11-storeyed castle is more than 300 meters high. It is home to houses, caves, pagodas, blockhouses, defense works and tunnels. The previously stylish caves are now seriously damaged. Few works of architecture remain intact, but Guge's appearance is still imposing.

Influential Figures in Tibet History

Who are the most influential figures in Tibet history? They are listed as follow.

Guru Rinpoche

Guru Rinpoche or Padmasambhava was an emanation of the Buddha Amitaba and a great yogi from the region that borders on present-day

Pakistan and Afghanistan. Admasambhava means "the Lotus-Born" in Tibetan. It was said that Guru Rinpoche appeared miraculously in the blossom of a lotus in Lake Danakosha, the "Ocean of Milk" in South West Oddiyana. When the king saw the child sitting on the lotus, he was filled with delight and invited him to the palace as his son and religious guide. The child was named Padmasambhava, the "lotus-born."

He brought Buddhism to Tibet in the eighth century and is affectionately called Guru Rinpoche. He spent more than 55 years in Tibet, manifesting countless wonders and is highly revered by all the schools of Tibetan Buddhism, and especially by the Nyingma.

Tsongkhapa

Tsongkhapa, whose ordained name was Losang Dragpa, was a famous teacher of Tibetan Buddhism and the founder of Gelugpa School of Tibetan Buddhism. His name means "The Man from Onion Valley" in Tibetan. Tsongkhapa was born into a nomadic family in Amdo Tibetan area in 1357. Today the location of Tsongkhapa's birth is marked by Kumbum Monastery.

Tsongkhapa was a great 14th century Tibetan Buddhist Master who promoted and developed the Kadampa Buddhism that Atisha had introduced three centuries earlier. His appearance in Tibet had been predicted by Buddha himself.

As a great teacher of Tibetan Buddhism, Tsongkhapa patiently taught the Tibetans everything they needed for their spiritual development, from the initial step of entering into a spiritual practice through to the ultimate attainment of Buddhahood. His followers became known as the 'New Kadampas', and to this day Kadampa Buddhists worldwide study his teachings and strive to emulate his pure example.

Fifth Dalai Lama

The fifth Dalai Lama, Ngawang Lobsang Gyatso was a key religious and temporal leader of Tibet. The fifth Dalai Lama was credited with unifying central Tibet after a protracted era of civil wars. As an independent head of state, he built the bulk of famous Potala Palace, established diplomatic relations with China and also met with early European explorers. He was the first Dalai Lama to become spiritual and political leader of Tibet and the greatest of all the Dalai Lamas.

King Songtsen Gampo

Songtsen Gampo was a great Tibet king of Tubo Kingdom. He was the first king unified Tibet in history. Together with his two wives, Princess Wencheng from Tang Dynasty of China and Princess Bhrukuti from

Nepal, Songtsen Gampo was credited with introducing Buddhism into Tibet in the 7th century.

King Trisong Detsen

Trisong Detsen is very important to the history of Tibetan Buddhism as one of the three 'Dharma Kings' who established Buddhism in Tibet. The Three Dharma Kings were Songtsän Gampo, Trisong Detsen, and Ralpacan.

Geography and Environment

Located in the southwest of the People's Republic of China, Tibet Autonomous Region covers an area of more than 1.22 million square kilometers, accounting about one-eighth of Chinese territory. Second only to Xinjiang Uygur Autonomous Region, it's equivalent to the total area of Great Britain, France, Germany, the Netherlands and Luxembourg. Tibet has a boundary line over 3842 kilometers, surrounded by Xinjiang and Qinghai on the north, Sichuan and Yunnan on the east, Burma, India, Bhutan, Nepal and Kashmir region on the south and west.

Qinghai-Tibet Plateau, known the roof of the world, consists of the Himalayas, southern Tibet valley, northern Tibet plateau and mountain and canyon area of eastern Tibet. It's also regarded as the third pole on earth in addition to the North and South poles.

Tibet has a total lake area of about 23.8 thousand square kilometers with over 1,500 lakes of different sizes scattering around valleys and mountains. And many lakes in Tibet are endowed with significant religious meanings. Lake Namtso, Lake Manasarovar and Lake Yamdrok are the three world-known holy lakes.

What's more, Tibet has a very limited amount of arable land and a visit to farmer markets or local farms around Lhasa must be an unforgettable experience. Get more info about Tibet agriculture and climate, and the elevation change in 7 major regions of Tibet.

The Elevation Change in 7 Major Regions of Tibet

If you've ever spent time looking at a map and, specifically, zeroed in on Tibet, you'd notice that it is a land in good company. Just look at its neighbours—it's flanked by such significant regions like Central China, India, Bhutan and Nepal, all areas which have been rapidly gaining popularity as of late. And that's not just at the hands of Asian descendants visiting their native land. No, the tourist population is largely made up of young, western travellers who are seeking adventure in a foreign land, and those that are on a spiritual journey who are looking to immerse themselves in this eastern world, with its ancient religions, myths, and philosophies

So, you may be wondering, why visit Tibet? With all this richness lying in these surrounding areas, what sets it apart? What does it have that they don't?

Geographical Features

There are innumerable contributing factors that make Tibet the special place that it is, but part of that lies in its unparalleled, utterly unique geography—and this is where we'll lay our focus for the time being.

So, what is it that's so interesting here? It's the incredible variety, from the high-altitude peaks to the subterranean valleys, and everything in between. The majority of the land consists of what is called the Tibetan Plateau, a very high altitude steppe—or grasslands, if you prefer—that is broken up by impressive mountainous regions and bodies of water.

Tibet is often divided into two dominant regions: the northwestern lake region and the southeastern river region. As will be discussed, the climate is vastly different from one part of the region to the next, with certain areas having fertile land and robust ecosystems, and others having a more deserted atmosphere.

Maybe, you're starting to wonder why this really matters for you. Well, as a traveller, you want to make sure you're visiting places that will give you the most bang for your buck. The trick to this is knowing what that means for you. If you grew up in flatlands like the Maldives, or Everglades Florida, a thrilling trip would likely involve mountaintops or deep ravines. But if you grew up in Colorado, where snow-capped peaks are everywhere you look, perhaps you'd be more charmed if you were to explore the luscious woodlands that Tibet has to offer. Similarly, whether you're going to most enjoy a populated region or a quiet region entirely depends on your background and what you want to get out of your trip.

So, if you're interested in visiting a fairly flat land that has a dry, windy climate, you should plan to visit the lake region. With a mere 4 inches of precipitation all year and no rivers, it is very desert-like here. This can be very exotic and rewarding if you come from, say, London or Paris and could really use a break from the rain, no? There are also some mountains found here, though they are much less frequent than in other areas. And if you've never seen a hot spring, this could be the place to change all that—although do keep in mind that when it gets really cold, they tend to freeze over. The soil also tends to get affected by the chilly weather—in essence, the permafrost renders it not very fruitful, so if you're looking for plant and animal life, read on!

The river region is the perfect counterbalance to the lake region. Featuring rich, fertile land and many narrow valleys, the area's known for being void of permafrost and well irrigated. What does that all translate to? It being the perfect place to explore new forms of life. Ever seen a snow leopard before? How about a high-altitude jumping spider? This is definitely the place to go to strike these off your bucket list. Plus, this region just also happens to contain the deepest canyon in the world, the Yarlung Tsangpo Canyon. Not bad.

Tibet's Regions: Altitude, Scenery & Star Attractions

It is the altitude that really makes all the difference here. Elevation affects climate, which in turn affects the ecosystem; and then the ecosystem affects our perception of the land, and whether we choose to visit it or not. Period. So let's dig into Tibet's various regions, by altitude and uncover what will suit you and your travel needs best.

Nagqu

When it comes to food, Nagqu is famous for its must-try dried meat and its healing aweto, also known as cordyceps. Aweto is traditionally used to strengthen the immune system, improve athletic performance and reduce effects of aging. It is also credited with enhancing liver function in those suffering from hepatitis B. Aside from this, Nagqu is known for its many festivals - don't miss its Herb Festival, Ghost

Exorcising festival, or the grandest of them all - Horse-Racing Art festival.

Altitude: 4500 metres

Climate: sandstorms, cold, average temperature is -6°C

Ngari

Ngari is known for being the home of the holy Mount Kailash and Lake Manasarovar. Also found here are five ancient monasteries: Zhabura, Chiu Gompa, Zheri, Zhozhub, and Tholing. The oldest is Tholing Monastery; its name even expresses this, with Tholing meaning "hovering in the sky forever." If you get the chance to go, you'll also get the fortune of baring witness to the precious, utterly well-preserved fresco paintings here.

Altitude: 4500 metres

Climate: monsoon, precipitation in summer, average of 19°C year round

Shannan

This second largest city in Tibet is most well-known for its Tashilhunpo Monastery, which has been revered for it being the seat of the Panchen Lama—a spiritual figure that plays a hand in selecting the next Dalai Lama.

Altitude: 3830 metres

Climate: highland, continental, dry year round (*except in Himalayan Mountain region)

Himalayan Mountain Region of Shigatse

Climate: dry seasons (October-April), rainy seasons (May-September), low temperature

Lhasa

The "Land of the Gods," as Lhasa is often referred to, is the provincial capital of the Tibet Autonomous Region. It is over 1300 years old and, as such, has become home to many important Tibetan landmarks over this time, including Potala Palace, Jokhang Temple, and Norbulingka Palace.

Altitude: 3650 metres

Climate: temperate, semi-arid, monsoon, sunny

Chamdo

The third largest city, following Lhasa and Shigatse, is known for its Galden Jampaling Monastery. This is has historically been an extremely impressive edifice, at one time consisting of five temples, which housed 2500 monks. Today's current version, which was re-built in 1917, is still able to house approximately 800 monks.

Altitude: 3256 metres

Climate: vacillating between humid continental and subtropical highland; warm and wet summers; dry and frosty winters; average annual temperature 9°C

Nyingchi

The prefecture with the lowest altitude in Tibet, Nyingchi is filled with beautiful slow-flowing bodies of water like the Niyang River, and a bountiful of mountains that extend from east to west. It's famous for its Peach Blossom Festival in the Spring—this is a must-see!

Altitude: 3100 metres

Climate: varied (including tropical, subtropical, temperate, boreal, humid & semi-humid); average temperature is 9°C; lots of rain between May and September that often results in landslides

Choose Tibet

So, if you've got the travel bug and are just itching to set out on your next adventure, why not visit a strikingly unique Asian land? One with impressive mountain ranges that reach up to 7500 metres in height, sprawling brackish lakes and rivers, and, not to mention, the highest plateau in the world—that is, the 4500 metre-high Qinghai-Tibet Plateau, aka "the roof of the world." Make Tibet and all its exotic glory your latest discovery spot, your very own Narnia, if you will.

So, what part of Tibet are you most excited to visit?

Agriculture and Climate in Tibet

Tibet, an autonomous region of China, is known as the "roof of the world", and rightly so. Set between the Himalayan mountain range to the south and the Taklamakan Desert to the north, the Qinghai-Tibet plateau is the highest natural plateau the planet has ever seen. The plateau stretches for around 1,000 km from north to south and 2,500 km east to west, giving it a total area of around 2.5 million square kilometers. Covering parts of Nepal, Kashmir, and China as well, the plateau sits at an average elevation of over 4,500 meters above sea level, and is the location of Mt. Everest, the world's highest mountain. It is also the location of Dolma-la, the world's highest pass, which is situated to the north of the holy Mt. Kailash, in Ngari Prefecture in the southeast. The pass, which forms part of the holy kora, or trek, around the mountain, sits at an elevation of 5,630 meters, and is the highest point of the trek.

Tibetan Climate in Different Regions

Climate in northern Tibet

The plateau is a high-altitude steppe, with an arid landscape interspersed with mountains and lakes. To the south and east the steppe gives way to grasslands that can support the nomadic herdsmen, despite the frost that covers the area for half of the year. As you move north and northwest the plateau gets progressively higher until it reaches the Changthang region in the far northwest. Here the average elevation is around 5,000 meters, and the temperature can drop to as low as -40°C in winter.

Changthang region is the least populated area in Asia, and third least populated in the world, after northern Greenland and Antarctica. The climate in the region is one that is wholly unique in the world. The climates differ in the various areas of the region, and the temperatures are just as varied.

Central and other parts of Tibet
The central area, around **Lhasa**, is more normal for an area that is still some 3,500 meters above sea level, and is good for tourists in the period from April to October. The temperatures range greatly from area to area, with an average temperature in Lhasa of 22°C-24°C. There is also very little rain in the region, even in the monsoon season. Annually, most of the rain falls in the period from July to August, although the average in most parts of Tibet is very low.

Southeastern Tibet has a gentler and more temperate climate than the rest of the region, with average temperatures of around 8°C. To the far west the average is below zero and the climate is more inhospitable.

Agricultural Economy

The Tibetan economy is mainly one of subsistence agriculture. With a very limited amount of arable land from crops, the main type of farming on the plateau is livestock, primarily yaks, sheep, and goats. These farmers are nomadic, and they manage their grazing using a mix of tradition, knowledge and environmental understanding. The nomadic farmers move their herds to different pastures depending on the season, which allows the pastures to recover and retain their fertility. With almost 75% of the TAR being pasture land, there is a natural wealth of animals from the lower pastures in the east to the high steppes of the west.

The croplands of the eastern areas are at very high altitudes in comparison to the rest of the world. Although the arable farmlands only account for 2% of the region's total area, they supply the essential grains for the population, in extreme altitudes and weather conditions. The farmers use a system of sustainability that is appropriate to this fragile environment. Crop rotation, mixing crops and fallow periods help to maintain good croplands in an area with a limited growing season. Although the main crop for the region for the last 3,600 years is barley - which is used to make the staple food, tsampa - other major crops have since been introduced, including rice, maize, millet, wheat and rapeseed. The main vegetables consist of cabbage, turnip, radish, potato, peas, beans and tomatoes, although these are expensive to ship to the remote western regions.

Crops planting and harvest season in Tibet

Crops in the region are planted normally in April following cultivation of the arable lands. The planting season starts with a traditional festival known as Nyatro. The farmers dress the yaks they will use for ploughing, and a celebratory meal is held on the land they will cultivate. On the following day the ploughing starts, then the barley and wheat is planted. As a community, the farmers have a system of working together to cover everyone's land, and get it ready for planting. The land is tilled using yak-drawn ploughs, and then hoed by hand to loosen the soil and remove large stones dug up by the plough.

Very few places in Tibet have irrigation systems, so they wait for the rains in mid-June for the crops to grow faster. Another festival is held at this time, known as Ongkor. The festival holds a small ritual kora around the farm for a better harvest. Crop ripening takes around 6 weeks after the rains have come, and the harvest starts from mid-August and runs into September. Harvesting is done manually, with groups of farmers working each others fields to make sure all the crops are gathered quickly. Harvest is done by hand, with short sickles to cut the stems. Any wheat and barley destined for long-term storage is bundled into sheaves and stored until needed.

Farmers Markets of Lhasa

In Lhasa, there are open-air markets that sell the produce of the local farmers. The bazaar-like areas in Lhasa's old town, around Barkhor Street, have a wide selection of imported nuts and dried fruits as well as tsampa, made from roasted barley, a dried yak cheese known as churpi and yak butter, etc. Locally made dried meats are popular with tourists, and you can also find many spices that have been imported from India. Originally established during the Qing Dynasty, the Tromsikhang market has over 300 years of history, and it sells hundreds of different local and imported products.

Something of interest to the visitors to the city would be the natural local crafts that are sold there. From hand made beads, to carved turquiose, beeswax and red corals, the sellers offer them to visitors that they think will buy them.

A visit to the farmers market - or one of the local farms around Lhasa if you have time - is an experience not to be forgotten. The traditional culture of the farmers and the selling of their produce is something not seen in many parts of the world anymore.

Environment of Tibet

Tibet is known as a holy land on the roof of the world. It is also considered as the late pure land on earth. Tibet had one of the most successful systems of environmental protection for the inhabited regions of the world. Formal protection of wildlife and environment through parks and reserves were unnecessary as Tibetan Buddhism taught the people about the interdependence of all living and non-living elements of the nature. Buddhism prohibits the killing of animals and advocates loving compassion for sentient beings and the environment.

Tibet Plants

Tibet is like a giant plant kingdom, with more than 100,000 species of high-grade plants. Many of them are rare and endemic. These plants include about 2,000 varieties of medical herbs used in the traditional medicinal systems of Tibet, China and India. Rhododendron, saffron, bottle-brush tree, high mountain rhubarb, Himalayan alpine serratula, falconer tree and hellebonne are among the many plants found in Tibet.

There are 400 species of rhododendron on the Tibetan Plateau, which make up about 50 percent of the world's total species. According to scientists, the Tibetan Plateau consists of over 12,000 species from

1,500 genera of vascular plants, which accounts for over half of the total genera found in China.

Tibet is also one of China's largest forest areas, preserving intact primeval forests. Almost all the main plant species from the tropical to the frigid zones of the northern hemisphere are found here. Forestry reserves exceed 2.08 billion cubic meters and the forest coverage rate is 9.84 percent. Common species include Himalayan pine, alpine larch, Pinus yunnanensis, Pinus armandis, Himalayan spruce, Himalayan fir, hard-stemmed long bract fir, hemlock, Monterey Larix potaniniis, Tibetan larch, Tibetan cypress and Chinese juniper. There are about 926,000 hectares of pine forest in Tibet.

Two species, Tibetan longleaf pine and Tibetan lacebark pine, are included in the listing of tree species under state protection. There are more than 1,000 wild plants used for medicine, 400 of which are medicinal herbs most often used. Particularly well known medicine plants include Chinese caterpillar fungus, Fritillaria Thunbergii, Rhizoma Picrorhizae, rhubarb, Rhizoma Gastrodiae, pseudo-ginseng, Codonopsis Pilosula, Radix Gentiane Macrophyllae, Radix Salviae Miltiorrhizae, glossy ganoderma, and Caulis Spatholobi. In addition, there are over 200 known species of fungi, including famous edible fungi songrong, hedgehog hydnum, zhangzi fungus, mush rooms, black fungi, tremellas and yellow fungi. Fungi for medical use include tuckahoes, songganlan, stone-like omphalias.

Tibet Wild Animals

The mountains and forests of Tibet are home to a vast range of animal life found only in Tibet. There are a variety of wild animals in Tibet, about 142 species of mammals, 473 species of birds, 49 species of reptiles, 44 species of amphibians, 64 species of fish and more than 2,300 species of insects.

Famous Tibet wild animals include Cercopithecus, Assamese macaque, rhesus monkey, muntjak, head-haired deer, wild cattle, red-spotted antelopes, serows, leopards, clouded leopards, black bears, wild cats, weasels, little pandas, red deer, river deer, whitelipped deer, wild yaks, Tibetan antelopes, wild donkeys, argalis, Mongolian gazelles, foxes, wolves, iynxes, brown bears, jackals, blue sheep, and snow leopards.

The Tibetan antelope, wild yak, wild donkey and argali are all rare species particular to the Qinghai-Tibet Plateau, and are under state protection. The white-lipped deer, found only in China, is of particular rarity. The black-necked crane and the Tibetan pheasant are under first-grade state protection. Wild yak is one of rare species particular to the Qinghai-Tibet Plateau and under state protection.

These rare and threaten animals include: the snow leopard, Tibetan takin, Himalayan black bear, wild yak (drong in Tibetan), blue sheep, musk deer, golden monkey, wild ass (kyang in Tibetan), Tibetan gazelle, Himalayan mouse hare, Tibetan antelope, giant panda and red panda.

Birds in Tibet

In Tibet, there are over 532 different species of birds in 57 families, which is about 70 percent of the total families found in China. Some of the birds include: storks, wild swans, Blyth's kingfisher, geese, ducks, shorebirds, raptors, brown-chested jungle flycatchers, redstarts, finches, grey-sided thrushes, Przewalski's parrotbills, wagtails, chickadees, large-billed bush warblers, bearded vultures, woodpeckers and nuthatches. The most famous being the black-necked crane called trung trung kaynak in Tibetan. Unfortunately, without the Tibetan sense of enviromentalism, several of these birds are threatened with extinction.

Forest in Tibet

Tibet's forests covered 25.2 million hectares. Most forests in Tibet grow on steep, isolated slopes in the river valleys of Tibet's low lying southeastern region. The principal types are tropical montane and subtropical montane coniferous forest, with evergreen spruce, fir, pine larch, cypress, birch and oak among the main species. Tibet's forests are primarily old growth, with trees over 200 years old. The average stock density is 272 cubic metres per hectare, but U-Tsang's old growth areas reach 2,300 cubic metres per hectare - the world's highest stock density for conifers.

Minerals in Tibet

Tibet also had rich and untouched mineral resources. Tibet has deposits of about 126 different minerals accounting for a significant share of the entire world's reserves of gold, chromite, copper, borax and iron. The former Chinese Communist Party Chair, Yin Fatang, reported that the world's largest supply of uranium was locked in to the Himalayan region of Tibet.

Rivers and Lakes in Tibet

Tibet is the source of many of the Asia's principal rivers, which include: the Brahmaputra (Yarlung Tsangpo), the Indus (Senge Khabab), the Sutlej (Langchen Khabab), the Karnali (Macha Khabab), Arun (Phongchu), the Salween (Gyalmo Ngulchu), the Mekong (Zachu), the Yangtse (Drichu), the Huangho or Yellow River (Machu) and the Irrawaddy. These rivers flow into ten countries such as China, India, Pakistan, Nepal, Bhutan, Bangladesh, Burma, Thailand, Vietnam, Laos and Cambodia. These rivers and their tributaries are the life-blood of millions of people in Asia. More than 15,000 natural lakes are found in Tibet and some of the prominent lakes are Mansarovar (Mapham Yumtso), Namtso, Yamdrok Yumtso and the largest, Kokonor Lake (Tso Ngonpo).

Tibet Local Customs

Tibetan customs and traditions are inextricably interwoven with **Tibetan Buddhism** and **unique Tibetan topography**. While travelling in Tibet, you'll find out that Tibet customs are also greatly influenced by Tibetan Buddhism. A good case in point is Weisang, a Tibet local custom that is observed on occasions like weddings and funerals by burning pine branches, cypresses and other herbal leaves around temples and monasteries to pray for peace, good harvest and prosperity.

Mani stones in different sizes and colors with Buddhist themes on are common to see on Qinghai-Tibet Plateau. Local people circle around Mani stones in a clockwise direction to show their sincerity to the Buddha and hope their wishes will come true one day. It's been told that where there are Tibetans, there are prayer flags. And its history can be traced back to the Bon tradition.

As you tour Tibet, a vivid picture of Tibetan customs and local life unfold before your eyes. When visiting Tibetans' family, you will how important the wooden bowls, Tsampa, yak butter tea, gutu and sweet tea are in Tibetans' daily life and how great Himalayas, sacred Namtso lake and alpine pasture play a part in shaping distinct nomadic customs.

From the biggest celebration, Tibetan New Year (or Losar) festival to numerous religious and secular festivals like Shoton Featival, Saga Saga Dawa Festival, Tashilhunpo Thangka Festival, Yushu Horse Racing Festival, you name it, they will definitely deepen your understanding of Tibetan culture and history and refresh your impression of real Tibet.

Let's learn more about diverse Tibetan customs, etiquettes and sports, funerals and relevant taboos, and be a Tibetan cultural expert before heading towards Tibet.

Tibetan Funerals & Relevant Taboos

Like with any other culture, Birth and Death in Tibet are two stages of life that are attached a lot of importance. There are a whole host of rituals and philosophies associated with birth and death in Tibet. This is directly related to the Buddhist and local animist culture there.

Tibetan Buddhists strongly believe in life after death and reincarnation.

In fact, the concept of death is so deeply interwoven in Tibetan culture that Tibetans try to spend their lives doing meritorious deeds and performing sin cleaning rituals in order to get a favourable rebirth.

Tibetans have an interesting take on death. They believe that death is not the end but the gateway to a different beginning. In Tibet, there are different ways of burial and different funeral customs according to this burial. This article will discuss them.

Sky Burial—the most sacred funeral ceremony in Tibet

Sky Burial- The first in our list is Sky Burial. Sky Burial is a very unique and rather macabre way of disposing the dead. It is not really a burial because the corpses are not buried anywhere. Instead they are left on very high, isolated places for vultures to devour. Yes, you read it right, Vultures eat the dead bodies. This method is primarily used by commoners.

Philosophy behind the sacred ritual
The reasoning behind this is that the souls of the departed can directly go to heavenly realms if left out in the open and at a high place. Another philosophy behind this is that the body is just a vessel for the

soul or consciousness; hence once the body has died it just has to be discarded like any old thing.

Vultures which eat the body are considered sacred. Tibetans believe that if a vulture eats the body, the soul was pure and has attained a good rebirth. There are certain rituals to this practise. When the body has died, it is kept outside the house for 3-5 days and monks chants mantras and sutras for the soul to migrate from death to the next life. Then it is carried away by the body carrier to a mountain top. There the body is bent into fetal position. A special smoke is released to signal to the birds that a body is available for feasting. Once the birds have finished eating, monks collect the remains and burn them. The ashes are then mixed with barley flour (Tsampa) and made into a broth which is fed to the vultures. This ritual is famous in the Drigung Monastery.

An interesting ritual in this is when the body carriers are carrying the body to the mountain and then dissecting them so the birds feed on the flesh, the body carriers never do this sadly. They instead laugh and tell jokes while doing this as they believe a light-hearted atmosphere will let the soul pass into next life positively.

Some of the taboos which Tibetans observe for this ritual are- Family members as well as strangers are not allowed to attend the vulture ceremony or witness the birds eating the bodies as Tibetans believe that this will bring them bad luck and also prevent the soul from passing on peacefully.

Stupa burial--a special burial for Tibet monks of high rank

Stupa burial is only used for the living Buddha, high ranking lamas like the Dalai Lama and Panchen Lama. When an important monk dies, his body is embalmed and then placed in the stupa where it will be worshipped.

When a Buddha or Dalai Lama or Panchen Lama dies, the body is embalmed using various things like camphor water, mercury water, saffron, and sometimes even gold flakes. All the internal organs are removed. It is wrapped in silk and put in a stupa. Butter lamps are kept burning day and night for weeks on end to show devotion. There are different kinds of stupa and the monk is assigned a stupa based on his rank. The different stupas are made of Gold, Silver, Bronze or Wood. The stupa type depends on the ranking of the lama.

Fire Burial- another unique funeral for prestigious Tibetan monks

Fire Burial is another type of funeral practise in Tibet. This is primarily meant for other high ranking monks (not Dalai Lama/Panchen Lama) and high ranking officials. The bodies of these people are cremated when they die. Generally after cremation the ashes are collected and scattered in a river or to the winds or buried underground. In some cases the ashes are kept along with some special beads, prayers books, chanting beads, etc. and worshipped. This is usually done only to monks.

Water Burial- common funeral of ordinary people

Water burial is not aspopular a funeral style as sky burial or even cremation. It is used for commoners and very low ranking people like beggars, the poor, etc. However this form of burial is more popular in the South of Tibet than in the north as vultures are not widely available

In water burial the body is wrapped in a white cloth and disposed off into a river, where it will be carried away by the waters. It is said to represent one's continuing journey in the waters of life or Samsara. The body is sometimes cut up first and then thrown into the water or it is just thrown whole. The body is eventually eaten by fishes and other life forms in the rivers. People in the south of Tibet have do not eat fish.

Tree burial- an extraordinary funeral for small kids

Tree burial is another bizarre form of funeral where the dead are buried in a coffin and the coffin is then hung on trees, far away from human habitation. This is practiced primarily in the Nyingchi region.

This form of burial is used only for children and aborted fetuses. In this, the body is cleaned with salt water, then it is placed in a fetal position. Then the body is placed in a wooden coffin or basket and this is hung far away from the village, usually in a dense forest. This is done as it is believed doing so will prevent the death of another child in the family. It is also kept far away from the view of the other children as it is believed that if other children view this, similar misfortune may befall them. The casket eventually disintegrates and the body falls to the earth, where it will decompose further.

The above listed practises are the main funeral and burial forms practised in Tibet. There are other forms too like earth burial and cliff burial but they are hardly practised anymore and are extremely rare to encounter. For our Tibetans, death is the beginning of a new journey not the end.

The Sporty Side of Tibet

When one imagines Tibet or Tibetans, the most common things that come to mind are peaceful and serene landscapes, calm people sitting on sidewalks drinking Yak tea or extremely religious and pious individuals. This is one of the most common misconceptions one has about Tibet. But, Tibet is a place which is much deeper and vibrant than you think, and spending ample amount of time here will help you see Tibet in a better light.

In fact, Tibetans are born sportsmen. Tibetan sports and games are closely related to their unique life on the plateau. Most games are played even today as a major influencing part of their culture. Thus making it essential to understand the sports they play as it also speaks greatly about the history and culture of Tibet.

Most religious festivals are often accompanied with sports and competitions, making it a colourful and joyous occasion. The most famous festival, the "Great Prayer", marks the Tibetans, playing various sports such as gun firing, arrow shooting, pony races, wrestling, etc. to name a few. These sports are played in the concluding days of the "Great Prayer". It is presided by the master of ceremonies, who are selected among the youngest officials who are at the onset of their career. This is a grand and adventurous occasion that shouldn't be missed to understand the history of Tibet on the sports they play. Some of the major sports played by Tibetans have been mentioned below:

1. Archery

This is a very popular sport that is played even today, in modern Tibet. This sport has been inspired by the art of hunting. There are many contests and challenges held every year in the sport of archery. The unique aspect of archery in Tibet, which sets them aside from the world, is the particular type of arrows used in the event. These Tibetan arrows are said to whistle as they cut across the air when shot from the bow.

This is one of the famous festivals held in the grasslands of Tibet. Here the archers are expected to compete and shoot targets. There are various sub-contests held which are short range shooting, long range shooting, and shooting when on a galloping horse, to name a few. This festival is a grand occasion and is said to last for three days. The festival is celebrated with great pomp, and is a must watch for one to understand the culture of Tibet.

2. Yak Racing

This sport is played as a subsection of the Horse Racing Festival in Tibet. Here, the locals compete to race small distances on the back of yaks. The spirit and energy seen during this event are close to nothing you've seen before. A common sight seen is, the rider of the yak often carries a whip of sorts, to make the yak move faster so as to win the race. The yak races are often only done for short distances, as the yaks perform well only for shorter distances, and they get easily tired when made to run for longer distances.

This is again played in the grasslands of Tibet. The yaks' head is decorated with red and other vibrant coloured flowers; their backs are caparisoned with decked saddles. One of the festivals, where one can see this sort of competition is in the annual Shoton Festival, which falls in the month of August each year. This sport is rather famous in Tibet, where people are seen performing dances and songs alongside the competitions. The winner of the yak races is given a "Khatag" which is a Tibetan scarf and a prize money to go with it, as well.

3.Horse racing

Horse racing is considered one of the oldest and most traditional sports of Tibet. This sport is held in the grassroots and agricultural regions of Tibet. The horses are made to run for an average of ten kilometres. The riders are often young Tibetans who are known to race without saddles on the backs of horses showing extreme horsemanship. The sport is considered so vital in Tibet, that there is also an independent festival to celebrate the event. It is known to last for over ten days. When the race is happening, in parallel one can see the locals wearing unique clothing, dancing and singing – their way of encouraging their riders to win the race.

The three most famous horse racing festivals in Tibet are:

1) The Yushu Horse Racing Festival

2) The Ngachu Horse Racing Festival

3) The Litang Horse Racing Festival

During these festivals, it makes for an ideal time for one to eat the local food and buy local herbs and spices. It is also known for the little shops which allow for one to buy the local handicrafts, jewelry and other such items. It is also known as an ideal time to get to know one another. This place is also infamously known, for individuals to have found their spouses during these festivals.

4. Wrestling

Wrestling is as old as time gets in Tibet. It is dated back to the times when people wrestled without any weapons as well. Wrestling was used as a means to close combat battles between tribes facing internal and external conflict. Various matches and tournaments are held annually, throughout the length and breadth of the country so as to find the nation's best wrestler.

5.Rock carrying

Rock-carrying is an interesting Tibetan sport. Here, individuals compete to find the strongest person amongst them. Though it was started as a part of manual labour, it gained momentum and became an attention-grabbing and entertaining competition where one could get a platform to show off their arm strength. It is particularly famous in the farming and herding areas of Tibet, during festivals and other gatherings. There are various types or categories in which one can participate.

According to the ancient folklore, rock-carrying first appeared in the epoch of Songtsen Gampo. It was also listed as one of the "Nine Sports" that all Tibetan men were to learn in their journey of life. Famous places, such as The Jokhang Temple, the Samye Monastery, and even the Potala Palace all contain murals and paintings portraying rock-carrying as an ancient and traditional sport.

6.Horsemanship

Horsemanship is a unique and exciting sport where riders are expected to carry or pick things off the ground while riding the horse. The objects they are required to pick are often ceremonial scarves. This presents an exceptional platform for riders to show their riding skills.

The riders are often seen wearing bright and fancy clothing. They are also known to decorate their horses as well. The other variant of the same sport is when riders are asked to shoot at distant targets while still riding at high speeds. This is a very well-known and revered form of sport in Tibet.

7. Tibetan tug of war

This sport isn't taken as seriously as the other ones, as it is considered more of a game, than a sport. It is often played non-competitively and for entertainment and recreational purposes. In this sport, two participants are asked to hold two ends of a rope. They are divided in the middle with a line; they are expected not to cross this line. The victor of the game is, one who on signal, pulls the other individual across the middle line that is drawn. Adaptions of the same game are seen in many parts of the world.

8. Gyiren—Tibetan Snooker

Tibetan Snooker is also termed "Given," or billiards without any ball arms. It is played without using a cue. The game originated from the lands on Kashmir, in India. Though it was considered the game of only the elite in the earlier days, the perception is slowly changing over time. The evenings are considered the best time to relax, catch up on some tea and play the game

With a magnificent natural landscape, Tibet, which is known as the "Roof of the world", is indeed an interesting place for one to catch up on outdoor activities and sports such as these.

Sky Burial in Tibet and Tibetan Funeral Customs

Sky Burial of Tibet (Celestial funeral)

Sky burial is simply the disposal of a corpse to be devoured by vultures. In Tibetan Buddhism, sky burial is believed to represent their wishes to go to heaven. It is the most widespread way for commoners to deal with the dead in Tibet.

Procedures of Sky Funeral Tibet

a. Preparation And Mantra Chanting

If a Tibetan dies, the corpse is wrapped in white Tibetan cloth and placed in a corner of the house for three or five days, during which monks or lamas are asked to read the scripture aloud so that the souls can be released from purgatory. The Family members stop other activities in order to create a peaceful environment to allow convenient passage for ascension of souls into heaven.

b. Body Dissection for Vultures to Eat

Later, the Family members will choose a lucky day and ask the body carrier to carry the body away to the celestial burial platform. On the day before the burial, the family members take off the clothes of the dead and fix the corpse in a fetal position. Specifically, the body is bent into a sitting position, with the head against the knees. At dawn on the lucky day, the corpse is sent to the burial site among mountains which is always far from the residential area. Then "Su" smoke is burned to attract condors, Lamas chant sutras to redeem the sins of the soul, and a professional celestial burial master deals with the body.

Sky Burial and Tibetan Buddhism

Practice of sky burial is closely related to philosophy of Tibetan Buddhism. Tibetans believe that if the vultures come and eat the body, it means that the dead has no sin and that his or her soul has gone peacefully to the Paradise. And the condors on the mountains around the celestial burial platform are "holy birds" and only eat the human body without attacking any small animals nearby. Any remains left by the holy birds must be collected up and burnt while the Lamas chant sutras to redeem the sins of the dead, because the remains would tie the spirits to this life.

Taboos of Vulture Sky Burial Tibet

Besides, there are a lot of taboos in the process of the celestial funeral in Tibet. Strangers are not allowed to attend the ceremony for

Tibetans believe it will bring negative efforts to the ascending of the souls. So visitors should respect this custom and keep away from such occasions. The family members are also not allowed to be present at the burial site.

Sky Burial Tibet Video

In addition to fierce and menacing vultures, the most intriguing part of sky funeral ritual is the body carrier (also known rogyapas or body breaker). They drag the dead body to the mountaintop and dissect it with blade. The whole process, as opposed to most people's expectation, is done not with solemn expression or deep sorrow on their face. Instead, body breakers chopped the body with laughter and smell as if they are doing other ordinary farm work, because Tibetan Buddhists believe that keeping a light-hearted atmosphere can help guide the dead to transcend from darkness to the next life. When the flesh is eaten up by vultures, the body breaker will smash the bone into pieces and mix it with tsampa (a staple food for Tibetans, made of barley flour) to feed the vultures.

Well-known Places of Sky Burials in Tibet

In fact, there are two well-known destinations for sky burial in Tibet. One is the Drigung Til Monastery, located in Maizhokunggar County around 150km east to Lhasa city. The monastery is embedded on the steep rock face of the cliff, overlooking the picturesque Mum Pa Valley.

Another prestigious one is Larung Gar Buddhist Academy, the world's biggest Buddhist academy. Situated Over 20 kilometers southeast to Sertar County, Garze Prefecture, Sichuan Province, Larung Gar Buddhist Academy is known for its massive Buddhist settlement and strong Buddhism study ambience, a must-visit destination for portrait and landscape photographers.

Other Tibet Funeral Customs

At the mention of Tibetan funeral customs, sky burial (celestial burial) would pop into our mind immediately. However, sky burial is not the only funeral ritual in Tibet. Greatly influenced by the Tibetan Buddhism and Bon Religion, funeral rituals practiced in Tibet are stupa burial, sky burial, fire burial (cremation), water burial, and internment. Cliff burial and tree burial are also practiced occasionally. The funeral services must follow the rigid hierarchy of ranks, sharp demarcation, and also mainly depends on the divination from Lama.

Stupa Burial

Stupa burial is the most noble and sacred funeral ritual in Tibet. Stupa is a Tibetan Buddhist religious monument and a sacred burial site. It is reserved for Dalai Lama, Panchen Lama or the Living Buddha. After the nirvana of a high Lama, the embalmed corpse is dehydrated and wrapped with rare medicinal herbs and spices. Gold flakes and saffron are scattered on the body in some cases.

Finally, the corpse is moved to the stupa and preserved for worshiping. Stupas can be elaborate or simple. It can be constructed of gold, silver, bronze, wood, or earth. The type of stupa selected is based on the ranking of the Lama.

Fire Burial (Cremation)

Cremation is considered less noble than stupa burial and is reserved for high monks and aristocrats. The corpse is seated on a stack of wood and straw poured with butter and burned. The ashes of the sainted monks will be put in a wood box or an earthen jar and thus and buried in the earth at home or on the top of a hill or in a piece of pure land. Or the ashes will be taken to the top of a tall mountain and scattered with the wind or into the river.

But the sainted Living Buddha or Lama's ashes usually is put into a small gold or silver tower some together with classical books, joss, musical instrument (used in Buddhist or Taoist mass), and treasures. The tower for worship is usually called mourning tower or mourning bone tower.

Water Burial

In water burial, the corpse is wrapped with white cloth and disposed into a river. There are two different views towards water burial. In areas where sky burial is the dominant practice, water burial is considered an inferior way to dispose of beggars and those with low social status. In places where vultures are not available for sky burial, water burial is widely adopted by commoners and the ritual follows a strict set of rules, sacredly and solemnly.

Earth Burial (Inhumation)

To the Tibetans, earth burial is the inferior form. Earth burial was prevalent in ancient times and was widely practiced by many ethnical clans. However, with the introduction of Tibetan Buddhism, sky burial became the dominant burial rite. Earth burial is now rarely practiced. Only those who suffer from infectious diseases or those killed by robbers or murderers will be buried in this way.

According to Tibetans, these bodies are not clean enough to be presented to the vultures. Earth burial indicates two meanings: One is to eradicate the spread of murrain. The other is to act as a way of penalizing the dead by putting it into the hell.

Tree Burial

This is a burial for children. It is commonly practiced in Nyingchi, southeast of Tibet. To avoid being seen by other children, the corpse of the child is placed in a wooden case and hung on a tree in a remote forest.

Cliff burial

Cliff burial is practiced in southern Tibet. The embalmed corpse is placed in a wooden box. The box is then placed in the cave off a cliff. The caves are usually 50-300 meters (164-984 feet) above ground.

Tibetan Tea Culture at The Roof of The World

Tibet, known as the roof of the world due to its high altitude, averagely over 3500m, enjoys distinctive tea culture. For hundreds of years, Tibetans have developed the habit of sipping tea. They can eat nothing except drinking tea. Let's travel to Tibet and experience the unique Tibetan tea culture at the roof of the world.

Tibetan tea culture consists of two traditional tea types. These are butter tea and sweet milk tea, which are found only in Tibet. Tibetans enjoy other types of tea as well, such as green tea, milk tea and boiled black tea. Many travelers heartily enjoy the peaceful environment of the local tea shops where they can relax and soak in the culture with an up close and personal experience.

Butter tea is the most popular one. Drinking butter tea is a regular part of Tibetan life. Before work, a Tibetan will typically down several bowlfuls of this beverage, and it is always served to guests. Nomads are said to often drink up to 40 cups of it a day. Since butter is the main ingredient, butter tea is a very warming drink, providing lots of caloric energy and is particularly suited to high altitudes. The butter also helps prevent chapped lips.

According to the Tibetan custom, butter tea is drunk in separate sips, and after each sip the host refills the bowl to the brim. Thus, the guest never drains his bowl; rather, it is constantly topped off. If the visitor does not wish to drink, the best thing to do is leave the tea untouched until the time comes to leave and then drain the bowl. In this way etiquette is observed and the host will not be offended.

The cups for drinking butter in Tibet are usually made of silver; some are made of gold. Tibetan people also use wooden bowls to drink tea. The wooden bowls are also set with gold, silver or copper. Furthermore, some Tibetan teaware is made of jade. The gorgeous and expensive jade teawares are handed down from generation to generation in a family. The teawares are also regarded as status symbols in Tibet

Tibet tea drinking has many rules. One such concerns a ritual performed by guests at another's house. The host will first pour some highland barley wine. The guest must dip his finger in the wine and flick some away. This will be done three times to represent respect for the Buddha, Dharma, and Sangha. The cup will then be refilled two more times and on the last time it must be emptied or the host will be insulted. After this, the host will present a gift of butter wine to the guest, who will accept it without touching the rim of the bowl. The guest will then pour a glass for himself, and must finish the glass or be seen as rude. Tea drinking and its accompanying rules have a long and important history tied directly to respecting others. Therefore it is wise to ask advice from your Tibet tour consultant about the proper etiquette for your specific situation.

Tibetan Marriage Customs, Wedding Ceremony in Tibet

Tibetan is a minority with unique culture in China. Tibetan marriage customs are also special. Wedding ceremony in Tibet is also different in different regions of Tibet. Here we just talk about the common wedding traditions in Tibet.

Proposal in Tibetan Marriage Customs

Proposal is the first step of marriage. Traditionally, if a man is interested in a lady, he will seek her age, date of birth and her zodiac attribute (i.e mouse, ox, tiger, rabbit, dragon, snake, horse, sheep, monkey, chicken, dog or pig). With all the information on hand, he will consult an astrologist to check if her attributes are compatible with his. If both zodiac matched, the fellow's family will choose an auspicious day and get a matchmaker to visit the girl's family for the formal proposal, with gifts such as khatag, yak butter tea, barley wine and other gifts. If her family agrees, they will accept the gifts. Nowadays, freedom of choosing spouse is also prevail in Tibet.

Engagement in Tibetan Marriage Customs

If both sides agree with the marriage, they will choose another auspicious day to sign an engagement. The ceremony will be held at the lady's house and should be participated by representatives of both families and the chief witnesses. On that particular day, the man's family has to send Khatag and other gifts to every member of the lady's family. Contents of the engagement are more about mutual respect and love, showing filial piety for elders, good morality or inheriting fortune in future, etc. After the witnesses check the duplicate betrothal contracts, they will sign the contracts with the seals of the two families and pass them to both sides. Finally the lady's family will hold a banquet to celebrate the occasion. At the end of the banquet, each guest will be presented with Khatag upon leaving.

Tibetan Wedding Ceremony

Before the wedding, another auspicious day will be chosen for the wedding ceremony by the groom's family. On previous day of wedding ceremony, the groom's side sent a suit of beautiful clothing and a hair ornament wrapped by silk to the bride for wearing. On wedding day, the groom's side will find a man with good status to take a group of people and colorful arrows decorated with mirrors, jades and jewels, along with a finely decorated horse of pregnancy whose color match the bride's birthpet to bride's house. The bride's side will offer Qiema as a ritual of farewell before the groom's side arrives. As greeting bride party arrives, a colorful arrow will be plugged on the bride's back and a jade will be put upon her head to show bride now belongs to the bridegroom's side. A bride maid from the bride's side is sent to escort her in the greeting party. When bride leaves, someone of the bride's family will hold a colorful arrow in one hand and a mutton leg in another, standing in any high place and shout out "don't take away fortune of the family" until the bride's greeting party is out of sight.

The convoy is usually led by the astrologist, who wears a white gown. He rides on a white horse and holds a picture of the Nine Courts and

Eight Diagrams. Following behind are the welcoming group, the bride, accompanied by a bride maid on her side, and finally members of the groom at the end. The whole team sings loudly all the way while the bride weeps due to her separation from her family.

On the way, the family members of bridegroom are waiting beside the road and toast to the greeting party for three times. If coming across patients carried, people who are dumping garbage or carrying empty basket, the greeting party deems it as bad omens. If so, monks should be invited to chant scriptures for removing ill fortune after wedding days. All greeting members are chanting XieQin in the proceed while bride is crying.

Before the arrival of the bride, the groom would have the gate decorated and a cushion of barleys laid in front of his house. The cushion is covered with a piece of colorful embroidered cloth, on the top of which are some kernels in the shape of the propitious swastika. His family members welcome the bride with chang and chemar (a propitious funneled box with barleys and Tsambas separately put inside and butter sculptures stuck onto).

Upon arrival at the groom's house, the bride has to tramp on the road with barleys and tea leaves, symbolizing the harvest she is bringing into the family. After accepting the Khatag presented by the groom, she enters the house. The bride and groom will then sit together in the living room to receive good wishes, Khatag and other gifts from guests.

Then the newly wed are sent to their room, where lamas recite sutras to bless them. The family holds a banquet for the guests. Friends and relatives will sing and dance to celebrate

During the night, they will play funny games to tease the couple. For some rich families, the wedding ceremony in Tibet could last as long as thirty days, but generally it lasts three days or two days.

Returning Home

Usually 3 or 6 months after the marriage, the newly wed will visit the bride's parents. The bride's family has to prepare barleys, swastika pictures and others to welcome them and exchange Khatag, yak butter tea, chemar and other gifts with each other. Only then is the whole wedding ceremony in Tibet considered completed.

Tibetan Etiquettes

Tibetan people are very kind, hospitality and easy-going. They have unique life style and charming Tibetan culture. In daily life, they follows special Tibetan Etiquettes. If you are planning a Tibet tour, you should know how to respect local Tibetans before travelling to Tibet.

Greeting Etiquettes in Tibet

If a Tibetan encounters a friend or an acquaintance, he will remove his hat and bow while holding his hat in front of his chest. However, if he meets an official, a senior, or a highly respected person, he should lower his hat as much as possible when he bows. The other person should show exactly the same courtesy in return. Although this custom is fading, it is still regularly used.

Presenting Khatag

Presenting Khatag (a white, loosely woven scarf) is very popular in Tibet. It is a traditional practice of respect and hospitality in Tibet, and will be appreciated by your host. People present Khatag when they visit parents, worship the Buddha, see somebody off, welcome someone home, and so on. Generally, the presenter holds the Khatag with both arms stretched out evenly before him, and makes a little bow. The receiver accepts it with both hands held in front of himself (but not overly stretched out) and immediately puts it on around his neck and wears it, because putting it down immediately is very rude. However, when presenting Khatag to seniors, the two arms should be raised up above the head.

When presenting a Khatag to people of the same age or younger, the presenter can tie the Khatag directly to their necks. It is interesting that some Tibetans even take a Khatag with them when they go out in case that they meet friends or relatmoives; and some Tibetans even seal Khatag in letters so that they can send their very best wishes. This custom is derived from the ancient practice of adorning deities with clothing and has evolved into a greeting of respect and caring.

Etiquettes of Visiting Monasteries in Tibet

When you pay a visit to a monastery, remove your hat as entering the temple. Generally, it is not necessary to remove your shoes, even though monks do that. Tourists are allowed to come inside while monks are chanting. Sit or stand in the rear, or walk clockwise around the room— unless it's a Bon monastery, in which case walk counterclockwise. Do not talk aloud or irreverent conversation. Do not photograph anything inside without permission (photography outside is okay). Don't touch the murals, butter sculpture, or other things you see displayed. Do not sit with the soles of your feet facing the altar or any other sacred object or person. It would be a nice gesture to add some money to the little piles of cash you see around, but it's not required.

If you have purchased butter or oil as an offering, spoon it into the lamps yourself. You may follow the lead of other pilgrims in bowing to various shrines, but if your heart isn't in it then it's quite acceptable not to. In general, it's okay to wander around the building, and you can go to the roof or enter any room that's not locked—however you should stringently avoid entering chambers on the roof of the monastery where monks may be in retreat. Don't worry a lot about committing faux pas in a monastery, because if you're about to do something wrong, and there's someone around, then they will stop you. Tibetans are really very good natured and will not take offense.

Tibetan Buddhist Etiquette

When Tibetans worship the Living Buddha, stupa s and pagodas, they prostrate. Devoutly, they raise their hands together high above their heads, take one step forward, lower their hands to the height of their forehead, take another step forward, lower their hands before their chest and take a third step forward. Then they kneel down and stretch themselves out upon the ground. After arising, they repeat this process. While they are performing prostrations, they chant sacred words, usually: Om Mani Padme Hum. Many pilgrims spend several years traveling from other provinces to Tibet performing prostrations each and every step of the way. Even though some people have died while on the road, it is never considered a pity as having traveled toward Tibet in this manner is a lifelong honor.

Being a Host or Guest

As a host, a Tibetan should always let the guest be first, no matter walking or talking. People must sit cross-legged as it is very rude to let the sole of your shoes or feet point towards other people. And a hostess or one of the family's children will pour a bowl of yak butter tea for the guest. The guest must wait quietly until the host carries and presents the bowl of tea with both hands and the guest takes the tea from the host in the same manner. Then, the guest can enjoy the tea and conversation. As a polite guest, one does not empty his bowl as a never empty bowl signifies lasting abundance. The host will add more tea to your bowl to ensure that it is never empty.

During festivals, a guest will be offered chang (a special Tibetan drink). Before drinking, the guest first lightly dips his third finger in the bowl, and upon withdrawing his finger from the bowl, snaps the liquid on the finger into the air. This should be done three times as a symbol of making a sacrifice to the sky, the earth and one's ancestors. Afterwards, the guest sips only once from the bowl, and then allows the host to fill it. This is also done three times, and the fourth time the guest drinks, he must empty the bowl. After this process is completed, the guest can drink as much as he likes. In fact, he must drink a lot or the host will think that he is not pleased with the treat or that he is very unfriendly. There is a saying that underlines the importance of this ritual: 'One bowl only will make good friends enemies.'

Etiquettes on Tibetan Funeral Ceremony

Tibetan practice what is known as Sky Burials are very private ceremonies where the family and close loved ones of the deceased pay their last respects. This practice is not familiar to most of us and is very unique. Even so, it is considered highly offensive to intrude upon a family at this time, including taking pictures.

Tibetan Courtesy

Tibetans are exceedingly courteous and have rules governing their relationships. For example, polite language is widely used in Tibet. Tibetans use it when they are addressing seniors, people with higher social status or people of the same age and same status. If they call someone, they will add 'la' after the name to show their respect. Some Tibetans still believe that photos can steal their soul and whether or not you agree, taking pictures of people without their permission can be intrusive.

Mystical Tibetan Funeral Practices

Tibet is a fascinating and unique place not just because of its charming landscape, profound culture and devoted people, but also its various mystical funeral practices. An integral part of Tibetan culture and religion, funeral rituals practiced there today are mainly the stupa burial, celestial burial or sky burial, water burial and cremation. Inhumation, cliff burial and tree burial are also occasionally practiced in some parts of Tibet.

Tibetan Buddhism, also known as Lamaism, has a history of more than 1,400 years since it was first introduced into Tibet during the reign of King Songtsan Gampo in the seventh century when Tibet was finally unified and Tibetan language created. Throughout its development, Tibetan Buddhism has absorbed features of Indian Buddhism, Tibetan Bon religion and Chinese culture, thus appearing to be far more mystical than other forms of Buddhism. Tibetan burial customs are based on Buddhist belief in reincarnation. Tibetan people are not afraid of death. They face death calmly because they believe death does not terminate a person's life, but indicates rebirth.

Under different influences, Tibetan funerals present the following features:

(1) Heavily influenced by natural environment. Distribution and evolution of different funeral practices vary very much in the natural conditions of the areas. That is, in the places where the forest resources are shout, celestial burial will be predominantly adopted, while cremation will be less practiced. In the dense woods area in Southeastern Tibet, cremation prevails. In the places full of gullies or

torrential rivers, water burial will be treated equally with celestial burial.

(2) Deeply influenced by Tibetan Buddhism. The concept, ceremony, rituals and practices of funerals have changed greatly since the introduction of the Tibetan Buddhism. Influenced by such Buddhist concepts as transmigration or rebirth, the aboriginal inhumation practices have been gradually eliminated. For smoother transmigration, there should be no trace left of earthliness. The body is no exception and should be thoroughly disposed, either eaten by fish and vultures or incinerated.

(3) As for the eminent monks, who themselves are incinerated, need not go through the procedures of rebirth like the commoners. So the grand living Buddha like the Dalai Lama or the Panchan Lama will be well treated with stupa funerals. In conclusion, the history of the Tibetan funeral customs can be divided in two parts, with the later part being strongly influenced by Buddhism.

(4) All manner of funeral practices are used in Tibet. Besides the five main ways, namely celestial burial, Inhumation or entombment, water burial, incineration or cremation and mummified or preserved stupa burial, etc. There are also other ways, such as cliff burial, tree burial

multi-person burial and stone coffin burial, etc. This nearly includes all funeral practices existing in the world.

Mani Stones in Tibet

When you are traveling in Tibet, it is very common to come across many mounds of stones almost everywhere, in monasteries, beside villages, crossing, along paths and on mountains. Some of the stones are inscribed with pictures or characters, with prayer flags stuck in the middle usually. Sometimes they are decorated with sheep and yak horns. They are Mani Stones used as the worship and rogation spots for the local Tibetans, especially villagers who have difficulty accessing to temples. Tibetan people build these unique works of art to show their piety to their deities and the Buddha's teachings.

Upon encountering a mani stone mound, Tibetan people circumambulate it clockwise as a prayer offering for health, peace, and protection. Some devout Tibetan will pick up a stone by the way and cling it to the forehead, while murmuring mantras at the same time. Then they will drop it into the mound. That equals to praying or murmuring sutra texts. Thus, the piles get into larger and larger massifs. The divine subjects such as heads, horns and wools of animals and even hairs of human can also be added to the mound. It is believed that the sincere wishes begged to the Buddha would come true one day by circumambulating the mound.

The world's largest Mani stone mound is located in Xinzhai Village of Yushu Tibetan Autonomous Prefecture of Qinghai province. Reportedly, the first Rinpoche (Living Buddha) of Jiana settled in Gujie Monastery in Xinzhai and built a Mani mound there. Also called Jiana or Xinzhai, Mani Stone Mound became bigger and bigger in the following 200 odd years, consisting of 2.5 billion stones. Tens of thousand Mani stone of the mound are particularly precious which are engraved with words of law, calendar calculation, art theory, sutra texts and Buddha carvings

Mani stones are regarded sacred as the sacrifice to the Buddha. In Tibetan area, Mani stones in different colors, shapes with different images and texts engraved can be seen everywhere. They showcase the artistic charm of Tibetan culture. Mani stone is called Man Zha in Tibetan, meaning Sanskrit mandala. In the vast land of Tibet with sparse population, Mani stone mounds become the prayer halls and shrines for local Tibetans

Another type of Mani Stone is the Mani Stone Wall inscribed with characters and pictures specially designed by the expert. The common designs are 'Om Mani Padme Hum' mantras, with images of deities, monsters, strong animals and other Buddhist themes decorated sometimes. These walls mainly stand near the temples, which illuminate their golden halls and stupas and add much holiness and blaze to the temples. The widely spread sculptures in Tibet are made in the form of shadow relievos. These include the sculptures in the steep cliffs in Lhasa, Shigatse and other areas

Nowadays Mani Stone has become a form of art in Tibet, and a group of specialists engaging in the sculpture has emerged as required. The Mani Stones are often considered as patron saints to be stored in the house or taken along when going out.

Mani Stone handicraftsmen are peasants or herdsmen in spring, summer and autumn. They only engrave stones in winter. Long ago, Buddha paintings, incantations and Buddhist mottos are the main content on those stones. Enlightened by pictorial sutras from other countries, mani carving with both inscriptions and images were also made for illiteracy folks. There are commonly two kinds of Mani mounds: one is piled by rocks of different sizes and the other is characterized by blocks and pebbles carved with inscriptions and sculptures, which are upbuilt in an undulating line

Qiema Box - Essential Mascot for Tibetan New Year

Tibetan people have the custom of making a "Qiema" box during Tibetan New Year, expressing the wish of good harvest and auspiciousness in the coming year. As an essential mascot for Tibetan people to celebrate Tibetan New Year or other important Tibetan festivals, Qiema boxes are made of wood and filled with colorful barley kernels, butter sculptures and tsamba (a type of bread mixed with ghee).

The method of making Qiema box is to put into each side of a two-tier rectangular wooden box, barley kernels and tsamba, with Qingke spikes and butter sculptures (beautiful molded flowers covered in ghee). In the middle, colorful flowers and highland barley spikes are stuck as decorations. The Qiema box with many carvings is also painted beautifully using colored ghee, usually featuring such figures which represent longevity and harmony. The Tibetans take Qiema as a mascot. Barley kernels are a token of good luck; and tsamba symbolizes health and a bountiful harvest for the new year.

When Tibetan New Year is approaching, every household is busy making Qiema boxes. Some also purchase them on market. During New Year, a Qiema box is placed on a Tibetan cabinet in each Tibetan family. A guest would first come to the Qiema and pick several ears of wheat and some tsamba, then hurl them in the air for three times to worship God, before sampling some of the tsamba

Qiema box is not only a kind of offerings, but also a kind of gift in Tibet. During Tibetan New Year, Tibetan people exchange Qiema boxes with friends and neighbors, expressing the best wishes. When you visit a Tibetan family, you can also receive a gift of Qiema

Tibet Traditional Wedding

Tibet Autonomous Region is an area where Tibetan people live in concentrated communities, constituting more than 95 percent of the population of the region. Tibetan people have many habits which are different from Han nationality. Today, let's talk about Tibetan wedding traditions.

Girls in Tibet are initiated ceremoniously into adulthood, selecting a 'lucky' date according to the Tibetan calendar. Her hair will be plaited from a single to many braids and she will begin wearing a colorful 'apron', indicating her availability for marriage and male friendships

Public gatherings are considered appropriate occasions for boys to meet girls. Romantic bonfires in the moonlight draw boys and girls together to sing and to worship. After a period of courtship and permission to marry has been granted by each family, an elderly gentleman is asked to propose the marriage to the bride-to-be's parents. According to tradition, only the maternal uncle of the girl has the right to approve. Suitable gifts are presented to the bride's family once approval has been given

he day before the wedding, the engaged are not allowed to see each other at all. During the day, monks pray for their marriage to dispel any bad luck. On the wedding day, a show man repeats Tibetan rhymed congratulatory words for the new couple. Then, it is the time for guests to show their best wishes to both the bride and groom by offering Khatags, or scarves. Then, the performances begin. During the show, the couple's parents and relatives toast with the guests. The evening ends with a toast made by the new couple

After the wedding, all the relatives, friends, old classmates and colleagues gather at the new couple's home and celebrate until that late night. In Tibet, a new couple is not allowed to leave their home for three whole days—a test for both of them as to the strength of the marriage. If they persist, then Tibetans believe that their marriage will last forever

Tibetan wedding ceremony is followed by a joyful wedding feast, which is liberally interrupted by many presentations of ceremonial scarves, blessings, and gifts — so many that sometimes the groom and bride are nearly buried beneath the large number of scarves tied around their necks!

And now more and more Han couples choose take wedding photos in Tibet, they think that a new kind of holy feeling. They also hope their marriage could blessed by god. If you are lucky enough, you can join a local wedding and celebrating with them

hatag, an Auspicious Symbol in Tibetan Culture

Khatag is a traditional ceremonial scarf used in Tibet and Mongolia. Offering of khatag is a well known Tibetan culture in greetings. Khatags are often offered in Tibetan Buddhism to Buddhist images or statues, holy sites, lamas and in certain rituals. It represents the highest respect to the recipient.

Khatag Colors

Tibetan people worships white color, believing it symbolizes purity, auspiciousness, sincerity, kindness, justness and prosperity. Thus, the Tibetan khatags are usually white symbolizing the pure heart of the giver, though it is quite common to find yellow gold khatags as wel

However, there is a special kind of khatag with five colors on: blue, white, yellow, green and red, respectively indicating sky, cloud, land, river and the God in charge of Buddha dharma. Five-colored khatag is very valued gift which can be given to the Buddha statues or intimate relatives. According to the Buddhism teachings, five-colored khatag is the clothes of Buddha. Therefore, five-colored khatag can only be presented in some special occasions.

Material of Khatag

Khatag is usually made of silk and it is loosely weaved. Khatag is a Tibetan word meaning silks in Tibetan language.

Presenting Khatags in Tibet

Presenting khatag is very popular culture in Tibet. People offer khatag when they visit parents, worship the Buddha, see somebody off, welcome someone home, and so on. While offering the khatag the presenter makes a little bow and the receiver accepts it with both hands held in front of them and immediately puts it on around his neck and wears it.

However, when presenting khatag to seniors, the two arms should be raised up above the head. When presenting a khatag to people of the same age or younger, the presenter can tie the khatag directly to their necks. It is remarkable that some Tibetans even take a khatag with them when they go out in case that they meet friends or relatives; and some Tibetans even seal khatag in letters so that they can send their very best wishes. This is one of the most popular customs in Tibet where all of the people follow it interestingly.

Don'ts in Tibet

Before travelling to some places, you may like to know the local customs in advance for a better and friendlier tour, so does your Tibet tour, especially when you try to visit some local Tibetan families, you should pay attention not to offend the Tibetans and show them your respect. Then, how to show your respect and not to offend them? Here are certain don'ts in Tibet you should know or are interested to know of Tibetan culture, which might be very different from your own

1. One's hands are not supposed to put on the shoulder of the other one when two long-time-no-see friends greet or chat with each other.
2. Don't touch the head of a Tibetan.
3. Don't step across or tread on others' clothes or put yours upper those of others. Never step across from one's body.
4. Don't step across or tread on the tableware.
5. Don't spit or clap your palms behind the Tibetans.
6. Don't kill any animals or insects in monasteries.
7. Don't drive away or hurt eagles, for they are holy birds for Tibetans.

8. Women clothes, especially, women pants and underpants are not supposed to be aired to dry in a place where people pass.

9. Don't whistle or shout or cry inside a house.

10. One can not sweep the floor or pour out the trash after some family member goes away from home, or the guests have just left away, or at noon or after the sunset, or on the first day of Tibetan new year.

11. Non-relatives can not mention the name of the dead face to face with the relatives of the dead.

12. The work that should be done this year must be done this year, such as knitting a sweater or carpet and so on.

13. One can not go to the house of others at twilight, especially when there are women who's going to give birth to a baby or have just given birth to a baby, or heavily ill people in that house, which especially applies to strangers.

14. Any property is not allowed to take outside home after the noon.

15. Two family members are not supposed to go out at the same time if they head for opposite directions. They should go outside at different time instead.

16. Tibetan women can not comb or wash their hair in the evening, neither can they go outside with their hair not being tied up.

17. Bowls with cracks or breaches should not be used to serve dishes

or tea for guests.

18. If you take some highland barley wine or butter tea to the Tibetan family as presents when you pay a visit to their home, the Tibetans may give something else from their own home to you as a present, or they'll leave some of your presents to you, and its not because they don't like your presents, it's just their custom.

Wooden Bowls Play a Key Role in Tibetan Culture

Wooden bowls play an important role in Tibetan culture and Tibetan people's life. In Tibet, every family has wooden bowls. There are always two wooden bowls in a common Tibetan family, a big one and a small one, the former for the father and the latter for the mother. Even to this day, the father's bowl is larger than the mother's. If a couple happens to visit another family, the latter will be sure to serve the wife tea in a smaller bowl than her husband; otherwise, it would be considered impolite. When you travel to Tibet, you can see most local Tibetan people, Tibetan pilgrims in particular, carry a wooden bowl if the leave their home. They use the bowl to drink butter tea, eat tsaba or other food and drink

A crack in the wooden bowl is regarded as a sign of ill luck, and the bowl must be replaced. Now that china bowls have become popular, every family uses them as spares for guests. If the edge of the china bowl is clipped, it is also regarded as ill luck and cannot be used, especially by the guests. They avoid drinking tea from a cracked bowl in the early morning, and if they should do so accidentally, those who believe in this taboo stay at home the whole day just to avoid disaster.

It is cold in the northwestern part of Southwest China's Tibet Autonomous Region and mild in the southeast. People wear leather robes in the northwest to keep out the cold, while pulu (a kind of vegetable fiber) woolen garments are adopted in the southeast. While the garments are of different materials, they are both very loose with very broad cuffs and are very comfortable to wear. In the day, when it is sunny and warm, one can push up the sleeves to cool down; at night, one can sleep in the same clothes.

Both leather robes and pulu woolen garments have a belt around the waist, and when the belt is fastened, the front part becomes a hollow pocket in which one can put many daily necessities. One dispensable article in the pocket of every traveler is a wooden bowl, as it is very important to use one's own bowl. An average wooden bowl is cheap but good, and common people can afford it.

In Tibet, everyone who leaves home for a trip carries a wooden bowl in this way. The wooden bowls of the balladeers are the largest and "can hold 4.5 kilo of butter tea." Whenever the balladeers perform in the open at fairs or in marketplaces, they place their wooden bowls at the side, asking for tips. Then, the wooden bowl has an additional use, to hold money or other things.

Monks also use wooden bowls. People who know the monasteries well can tell which monastery the monk is from based on the shape of the bowl. The iron-club lamas always move the bowl from one hand to the other playfully, which is quite dazzling. In religious meetings, when the iron-club lama keeps order, his wooden bowl is an emblem of authority that is used to knock the head of those who do not observe the order, and they dare not respond.

Clergy and laypeople making obeisance to the Dalai Lama in the morning were usually awarded three bowls of butter tea. While they listened respectfully to the Dalai Lama or the prince regent, they sipped the butter tea from their bowls constantly.

When a person dies, the other family members fill the wooden bowl that he or she used for butter tea and place it before the corpse. On the seventh day after the sky burial, the family as well as relatives and friends follow the priest in charge to the bank of the Lhasa River to hold a ceremony wishing the dead person's spirit safety and peace. In the ceremony, they lay the wooden bowl in front of the dead person before them and repeatedly fill it with tea to wish the person a good voyage. Finally, they pour the tea out of the wooden bowl, clean it, and give it to the priest. After that, the bowl belongs to the priest. This is a rule in the burial custom: The priest in charge of the celestial burial possesses the bowl every time after the dead body is buried. If the family wants to keep the dead person's wooden bowl as a memento, they must buy it from the priest.

When you travel to Tibet, you can buy a wooden bowl as a souvenir. Barkhor Street is the best place for travellers to buy souvenir. You can find all kinds of local Tibetan handicrafts on this busy street.

Yak Racing, a Spectator Sport in Tibet

As a traditional sport in Tibet, yak racing is a spectator sport held at many traditional festivals in Tibet, such as the annual Shoton Festival which usually falls in August every year. Yak race can be one of the most entertaining parts of a Tibetan horse festival, in gatherings which integrate popular dances and songs with traditional physical games.

Each of the competitors, which commonly number 10 or 12, mounts his yak, and the yaks run towards the opposite end of the race course in a sprint. Yaks can run surprisingly fast over short distances. The winner is usually given several khatag (a traditional Tibetan scarf) as well as a small amount of prize money. Yak racing is also known to be performed in parts of Kazakhstan, Kyrgyzstan and in Pamir in Pakistan

During traditional festivals of Tibet, the people dress in their best finery and sing and dance to celebrate the banquet. At the capital of Tibet, Lhasa hugs lots of yak-racing master-hand from all around Tibet. The yaks' massive heads are adorned with red flowers, their backs caparisoned with ornamented saddles. The yak jockeys' whip hands fly as they urge their mounts still faster towards the finish line

At Yushu, another Tibetan area in Qinghai Province, yak racing has became an integral part of the Yushu Horse Festival and the nineteen-day Darma Festival in Gyangtse, and a comic highlight of the Damxung Horse Festival also known as the Dajyur.

Yak racing is also a common sport in the farming and stockbreeding areas on the grand Tibetan Plateau. They hold yak racing events annually to celebrate the good harvest, and they pray for good weather during the coming year

Witness to a Sky Burial in Tibet

Sky burial in Tibet is extremely mysterious for most people because strangers are usually not allowed to watch sky burial ceremonies in Tibet. So this mysterious custom in Tibet intrigues more and more people's curiosity. If you are lucky to get a chance to witness a sky burial in Tibet, please respect local custom. Do not get close to the sky burial site, take photos and ask any questions on site. Just stay quiet.

On the steps in front of Drigung Monastery, a dozen monks chant. Before them on the courtyard flagstones lies a body, wrapped in white cloth, which was carried in on a stretcher an hour ago. The monks are praying for a spirit that was once present here, but now is emancipated from its former home. It is the third such visitor today, for Drigung Gonpa has a profitable but gruesome specialty: disposal of the dead

My team and I arrived here last night, after a long day's drive from Lhasa to Meldor Gungkar County in Central Tibet. Drigung monastery is on a steep hill, overlooking our camp. Above the religious complex is a site for "sky burial," a term meaning disposal of a corpse by allowing it to be devoured by birds. The birds, which are summoned by incense and revered by Tibetans, cast their droppings on the high peaks. Sky-burial is practiced all over the plateau, but Drigung is one of the three most famous and auspicious sites.

After the chanting is over, we walk up a well-trodden path to a high ridge, keeping a respectful distance behind the funeral party, which has come all the way from Lhasa to discharge this final duty to their departed friend. The charnel ground, or durtro, consists of a large fenced meadow with a couple of temples and a large stone circle of stones at one end where the ceremony takes place. Prayer flags hang from numerous chortens, and scent of smoldering juniper purifies the air. Vultures circle overhead, and many more are clustered on the grass, a few meters from the funeral bier

Tibetans practice several forms of disposal of the dead, but sky burial (celestial funeral)is the most common method and indeed a very practical one in a land where fuel is scarce and the earth is often too hard to dig. For me, this is an extraordinary opportunity, for these days not one visitor in five hundred is privileged to witness the ceremony I'm about to see. But I am apprehensive, too, wondering how I will stomach the sight of death.

Men in long white aprons come out, and unwrap the corpse, which is naked, stiff, and swollen. The men hold huge cleavers, which are in a few strokes whetted to razor sharpness on nearby rocks. The bright sun and clear blue sky diffuse somewhat my ominous feeling. The coroners themselves, are not heavy or ceremonial, but completely businesslike as they chat amongst themselves, and prepare to start.

Tibetans believe that, more important than the body, is the spirit of the deceased. Following death, the body should not be touched for three days, except possibly at the crown of the head, through which the consciousness, or namshe, exits. Lamas guide the spirit in a series of prayers that last for seven weeks, as the person makes their way through the bardo—intermediate states that precede rebirth

As the first cut is made, the vultures crowd closer; but three men with long sticks wave them away. Within a few minutes the dead man's organs are removed and set aside for later, separate disposal. The vultures try to move in and are prevented by waving sticks and shouts. Then, the cutters give a signal and the men all simultaneously fall back. The flock rushes in, covering the body completely, their heads disappearing as they bend down to tear away bits of flesh. They are enormous birds, with wings spanning more than 2 meters, top-feathers of dirty white, and huge gray-brown backs. Their heads are virtually featherless, so as not to impede the bird when reaching into a body to feed

For thirteen minutes the vultures are in a feeding frenzy. The only sound is tearing flesh and chittering as they compete for the best bits. The birds are gradually sated, and some take to the air, their huge wings sounding like steam locomotives as they flap overhead. Now the men pull out what remains of the corpse—only a bloody skeleton—and shoo away the remaining birds. They take out huge mallets, and set to work pounding the bones. The men talk while they work, even laughing sometimes, for according to Tibetan belief the mortal remains are merely an empty vessel. The dead man's spirit is gone, its fate to be decided by karma accumulated through all past lives

The bones are soon reduced to splinters, mixed with barley flour and then thrown to crows and hawks, who have been waiting their turn. Remaining vultures grab slabs of softened gristle and greedily devour them. Half an hour later, the body has completely disappeared. The men leave also, their day's work finished. Soon, the hilltop is restored to serenity. I think of the man whose flesh is now soaring over the mountains, and decide that, if I happen to die on the high plateau, I wouldn't mind following him

Sweet Tea, Tibetan People's Coffee

n Tibet, sweet tea is just like Tibetan people's coffee, refresher of leisure time in Lhasa for locals and travellers to Tibet. The sweet tea houses in Lhasa are warming up with the arrival of locals and tourists in pairs or groups when night falls. In Tibet, no morning can happily pass without tea, usually the buttered tea, while no lunch is dainty without sweet tea. Sweet tea to Tibetan people is a drink just like coffee to the Westerners — a drink to wake up and start the day.

Sweet tea, means "Qiabadi" in Tibetan, is made of black tea, milk and white sugar, serving as refreshment. Sweet tea houses can be seen everywhere in Lhasa — no matter when taking a ritual walk around the magnificent Potala Palace or going shopping in the Barkor Street. Usually, the sweet tea house in Lhasa opens at 7:00 am, and closes up at midnight when business is good.

GuangMing Gang Qiong Tian ChaGuan is one of the most famous teahouses on Beijing Middle Road in Lhasa. Strong Tibetan flavor is pervading over the teahouse: colorful patterns of the eight auspicious symbols are painted on the yellow wall, traditional Tibetan rugs are put on the wooden desks and white khada are presented to a statue of Buddha on the counter. A pot of sweet tea, enough for four drinkers, costs 6 yuan at GuangMing Gang Qiong Tian ChaGuan

I am a regular customer here. SometimesI spend the whole day here with my friends." Tshe Sgron said, the locals like to go to the same teahouse even though they have to queue up. Young Tibetans are also patrons of the teahouse, where they can have a gathering with their friends.

Moreover, the sweet tea house also serves as a chess-and-card room for men. Tibetan men like to play xiu (a traditional Tibetan game of dicing, and players can "kill" each other in the game) at the teahouses. Tshe Sgron said the game is only for men in Tibetan area

The atmosphere of the teahouse is livening up by tea and wine. When Tibetans have no other place to go, the sweet tea house is a good choice to kill time as it also offers Tibetan staple food including zhaba and other Indian and Nepalese style food.

Replacing Valance on Tibetan New Year's Eve

Tibetan people use colorful valances to decorate the doors and windows of their houses. The colorful valances dance with wind and make the building more attractive. Replacing valance on Tibetan New Year's Eve also becomes a custom in Tibet.

Tibetan New Year is the most important festival in Tibet. It is usually celebrated in late January or early February at the time of the new moon. Tibetans begin preparing for New Year's Day early in the twelfth month according to the Tibetan calendar. Besides food preparation, each household has to get ready a five-cereal container which is a rich-carved colorful wooden box with fried highland barley mixed with butter inside and flowers made of butter and green shoots of highland barley above. This is done to pray for a bumper harvest and better life in the coming year. They also make fried wheat dough mixed with butter in various shapes as religious offerings and also for visiting guests

When Tibetan New Year approaches, you can find many venders on the Barkhor Street begin to sell valances. Piles of colorful valances can be seen on the floor. Replacing window and door valances implies good luck. If they do not replace the valance, it means the family is confronting with misfortune.

On the eve of the Tibetan New Year, Tibetans clean up their houses, change door and window valances, set up brand-new prayer flags on the roof and paint patterns symbolizing eternity and good luck on the gates with lime. In the evening, all family members reunite together and an "auspicious dinner" is offered. This dinner's main meal is dough drops known as Gutu in Tibetan, which include stone, wool, hot pepper, charcoal or coins inside. These items are said to be able to foretell the nature of and future fortunes of the person who eats them. The second day of Losar is a day for visiting friends and going to entertainments

Weisang, Tibetan Households' Custom

Weisang is a Tibetan household's custom of burning offerings to make cloudy smog, hence this kind of praying is also called smoke offering. "Wei" means simmer in Chinese. 'Sang' is a Tibetan 'ritual fireworks'. There is a variety in selection of material for Weisang, like branches pine and cypress, leaves of herbs such as Artemisia argyi and heath. It is said that the fragrance in the smoke produced during burning the pine trees and cypresses, can not only bathe unlucky and dirty things of ordinary people, but also aromatize the palace of mountain god who will be pleased after smelling the aroma. Therefore, Tibetan people pray for good fortune, good harvest, peace and prosperity by this way

Weisang is an ancient and widespread Tibetan customs. In addition to selection of cypress trees, it is also used along with wormwood and other herbs and heather leaves. There is a certain choice and a fixed ritual of Weisang ceremony: first cypress trees and herbs piled up in the hills or the river of mine on the ground, put the middle of roasted barley flour or grain, and then sprinkle a few drops of water lit by Sishen. Tibetan Weisang ceremony held on many occasions, such as the bumper harvest, attack enemies, beat the opposition, peace and prosperity, weddings and funerals, road safety, illnesses and sickness and so on.

According to the legend, Weisang came from the ancient tribe custom of welcoming brave fighters returning in triumph. In suburb, in order to clean out the dirt and dust on the fighters, people burned herbs and a pile of cypress branches, which will be dipped in water and then sprinkled to the brave fighters. By this way, the ancestors of plateau sacrificed gods, prayed for peace and victory, and gradually took this way as the main way to communicate with gods. Commonly, in ordinary days, Tibetans have the habit of Wei-Song, for example, every morning, in front of the gate, families burn some cedar branches matched with herbs to eliminate the evil and purify the air.

When there is a woman in the postpartum period, people will burn a heap of yak dung in front of gate to warn off the passers. Then people will pile up a scree pile, if a boy was born, people would pile up more chalk screes; if a girl was born, people would use other kind of screes and Wei-Song nearby the scree pile to get rid of the filthy atmosphere produced by procreation.

In the new year of Tibetan, coming back from the ceremony of expelling the evils, before entering home, people have to burn the mulberry branches to exclude the evils thoroughly.

If you go to visit temple to see who is practicing Buddhism solitarily when you are travelling in Tibet, you have to use the prepared mulberry branches in front of the temple gate to bathe, lest polluting the pure environment.

Gutu, Tibetan New Year Reunion Dinner

Gutu is a special dinner Tibetan people have on December 29 on Tibetan calendar to dispel ghosts, hanker for happiness and welcome Tibetan New Year. On December 29 of Tibetan lunar calendar, when it is dark, every family member is seated according to their seniority in the family tree and eats Tuba, which is a ceremony called "Gutu" to drive evil away and can be traced back to Tibetans' rituals. This is a very grand ceremony, and in Tibetan language, Gu means nine (for 29), and tu means Tuba

On this day, people prepare a very special dinner called "Gutu". For dinner people usually eat congee of barley or soup of Zanba. The special dinner "Gutu" consists of nine foodstuffs, barley flakes, peas, dough ball soup, radish and etc. To add to the festivity of the scene, people choose some symbolic things and stuff them into the wheat paste balls. Some symbolize luck and some symbolize different personalities. The stuffed paste balls and the dough balls are cooked together in a pottery pot into delicious soup. Before they eat Gutu soup, everybody rubs some parts of his body with a wet paste ball uttering these words like "Ah, the sufferings, pains and diseases all go away from me.

What a family member eats predicts his/her luck of the coming year. All the family member sit together and discuss what they are eating and their luck and wish of the New Year. It is really a very happy and peaceful scene. If you are just travelling in Tibet around Tibetan New Year, just join local Tibetans' new year dinner. You will be welcomed.

Another ceremony comes after the special dinner, that is, ghost-dispelling. Every household in the village lit firecrackers and torch made of straw, and yell "come out, come out" while running out of their houses to an intersection of their village. They would throw the torch and remained gutu at the intersection, which means that they have dispelled all the devil in their house and a good new year is coming

Why Tibetan People Worship Yak Head

When you are travelling in Tibet, you can see Mani stones everywhere. Sometimes, there are yak heads carved with Tibetan paternoster on the Mani stones. What are the yak heads used for? For Tibetan people, do the yak heads have any meaning? Why Tibetan people worship yak head?

The Yak is a long-haired bovine found throughout the Himalayan region of south Central Asia, the Tibetan Plateau and as far north as Mongolia and Russia. In addition to a large domestic population, there is a small, vulnerable wild yak population. In the 1990s, a concerted effort was undertaken to help save the wild yak population.

Customs and traditions aside, yak occupies an important place in the lives of the nomadic Tibetans. For them, yaks are so valuable that they call these animals "Norbu," meaning treasures. Yaks also find their way into artwork, such as monastery murals and rock carvings. On the street of Lhasa, you can find many vendors selling yak heads carved with Tibetan paternoster as artware. Some people would use yak head to decorate their house.

According to classics of the Bon religion, yaks came from heaven to the top of Gangdese Mountain. Of the Buddhist warriors, one had a yak's head.

Mysterious as the desolate Mexico Valley, the primitive Tibetan plateau with simple Tibetan people also attracts countless visitors from other places. As we all known, Tibetan people is an ethnic group with its own language, characters, customers and religion. Receiving more and more focus from all over the world, this unique nation arouses more and more people's interest, artists in particular. Flocks of artists, poets, writers, photographers, painters and film makers rush to Tibet to find inspiration from this mysterious land. Except bringing their own works back home, they also bring back a yak head as a souvenir so as to show off their pilgrimage journey.

In fact, when travelling on the last pure land on earth, you can find weathered or new-placed yak heads on the top of a hill, or on the bank of a river,or under an altar, even around monasteries, at the top of the gate of a village and so on. These rough, mysterious and powerful heads are so attractive for artists. Howerver, for local Tibetans, yak means mor

You know, there were no vehicles in Tibet in the past. Animals are what they are used as vehicles. Yak is on the earliest animals that Tibetan people have tamed. Due to their quick adaption to the cold highland and moderate temper, yaks were chosen as means of transportation in remote areas of Tibet. Therefore, yaks were reputed as the "boat on the plateau". But why Tibetan people worship yak head? I think it is because yak offers Tibetan people food by its meet and impact Tibetan people by its character

Tibetan Adult Ceremony for Girls

Traditionally, a Tibetan girl is considered as an adult when she is seventeen years old. A special Tibetan adult ceremony for girls, "Dai Tou", is held for her on a good day.

"Dai Tou" is a common expression for getting married. However, during this ceremony, it is not a real man that is married to the girl. It is said that the girl is supposed to hold the wedding ceremony with the blue sky above people's head. Because the girl is married to the blue sky, this ceremony is also called "Dai Tian Tou" ("wearing the head of the sky"). In fact, the ceremony of marrying the sky is the ceremony showing that young Tibetan women have entered adulthood.

In pasture areas of Tibet, a Tibetan girl only has two braids in their childhood, three braids at thirteen to fourteen years old and five or six braids at fifteen or sixteen years old. When she become an adult, she will have dozens of braids.

On the adult ceremony, her parents will invite a lucky girl with the same age to wear her hair in dozens of braids, which means that she is old enough to get married. Then the girl will wear the decoration of Patsu and the colorful skirt of Bangdian. Later, the girl's parents, relatives and guests will present her Hadas on congratulation. When the ceremony is over, the girl followed by three or four relatives, goes to the temple to worship the Buddha statue. After they come back, the family will provide a rich dinner for the guests.

After this ceremony, girls can identify themselves as adults and can have social contacts with people. They could have love relationship and take their beloved boyfriends home as they will. To have a child is acceptable for adult women in the community. Women after the ceremony can either get married or stay at her parents' home forever. Women can ask their lovers to become sexual partners. Unmarried women can live with their sons and daughters and form a matriarchal family

Tibetan Birth Ceremony

Tibetan birth ceremony is called Pang-sai in Tibetan language. The Pang-sai is actually a cleansing ritual aimed at cleansing the child from the journey into this life. "Pans" means fowls and "sai" means cleaning away in Tibetan. The Tibetans believe newborn babies come to the world alongside fowls, and a ceremony should be held to wipe them out so that these babies would be able to grow healthily and mothers recover soon.

Tibetan birth ritual, evolved from a Bon religious ritual to worship the God, have been going on for more than 1,500 years. When a baby is born, two banners will be placed on the roof eaves, hanging from the edge: one to ward off evil to protect the child and one to attract good fortune. However, the actual celebration does not commence until the third day of the child's life, or fourth for a girl child. It is probably because in old times the children did not always live this long in Tibet, which is high in altitude, but if they were still ok by three or four days, they would usually survive normally

Many people may journey from other places to take part in the birth ceremony. They bring gifts of food and clothing. Buttered tea, barley wine, meat, butter and cheese are presented to represent wishes for an abundant life. New clothing and wonderfully colored scarves are presented to represent shelter for life. Scarves are also presented to the parents to carry good wishes. As soon as they enter the house, they present hada scarves to the baby's parents and then the baby. This is followed by toasting, presenting gifts, and examining the baby while offering good wishes. Some families throw in a pancake feast to entertain the visitors

A visit by a monk from a local monastery or one of the families will insure that the child will develop wisdom. The monk(s) brings religious banners and leads in worship rituals in which everyone participates. Every day, there is family and visitors party for a week until the naming ceremony, but nobody comes into the house or see the child, except immediate family and the monks. The rest of the people are served and celebrate in the courtyard, which is usually partly covered and offers a warm fire. It will be a month before anyone outside of the family or the monks touches the child.

The newborn baby is not given a name until the end of the birth rituals. Generally, a Living Buddha or a prestigious senior villager is invited, but there are also cases when the baby is named by his/her parents. No matter who names the baby, the naming is performed in accordance with the will of the baby's parents for auspiciousness.

When the baby is one month old, a ritual is held on an auspicious day to take the baby out of the home. Before leaving, black ash taken from the pot bottom is used to blacken the baby's nose to ward off evil. Generally, the baby, donned in new clothes, is taken to the monastery for worshipping the Buddha and also for blessing.

Ritual Walk Season in Tibet – Saga Dawa Festival

The whole fourth Tibetan lunar month is the ritual walk season in Tibet when Tibetan people celebrate Saga Dawa Festival by ritual walks around sacred sites, like temples, holy mountains and lakes.

Saga Dawa is the entire fourth month of the Tibetan lunar calendar and is the holiest time of the Tibetan year and a peak time for pilgrimages. The Saga Dawa Festival lasts from April 1 to April 30 on Tibetan calendar, but April 15 is the grandest day. The highlights of Saga Dawa Festival 2017 will fall on June 9, 2017 in solar calendar. (See our predesigned Saga Dawa Festival Tour 2017)

The seventh day of Saga Dawa is the day of the historical Buddha's birth for Tibetans. However, the Buddha's birth, enlightenment and entry into Nirvana at his death are observed together on the 15th day of Saga Dawa. "Saga" is the 28th constellation named Di and "Dawa" means "month" in Tibetan. The birth and the attainment of nirvana of Sakyamuni is believed on April 15, the fifteenth of the fourth month on Tibetan calendar, so more Buddhist ceremonies are held in this month.

Lhasa is a centre for celebrating Saga Dawa Festival. During the period of the Saga Dawa Festival, hundreds of thousands of believers gather in Lhasa to take ritual walks while participating in ceremonious activities including fasting, freeing captive animals, alms giving, etc. Tibetan Buddhism believers burn mulberry branches in the incense-burner in front of holy temples and mountains

Another centre of Saga Dawa Festival is Mt. Kailash. During the Saga Dawa Festival, Mt. Kailash would witness thousands of pilgrims. For over a thousand years pilgrims have flocked to Mt Kailash to replace the Tarboche flagpole, a huge pole that stands on the Kailash kora (hiking circuit), south of the mountain. The ceremony is led by a lama from the nearby monastery and Tibetans and Buddhists gather here to attach their prayer flags, to pray and to help erect the flagpole

History of Prayer Flags in Tibet

Where there are Tibetan prayer flags there are Tibetan people. The colorful prayer flags are the patron of Tibetan people. The history of prayer flags in Tibet can be traced back thousands of years to the Bon tradition of pre-Buddhist Tibet according to some lamas.

The primary colored plain cloth flags were used in healing ceremonies by followers of Bonpo. Each color had a different primary element - earth, water, fire, air and space which are the fundamental building blocks of both our physical bodies and of our environment. We need to keep the five elements in harmony to maintain healthy. When someone gets ill, the colored flags are properly arranged around the patient to harmonize the elements in his/her body. The prayer flags were also used to help appease the local gods and spirits of the mountains, valleys, lakes and streams which were believed to cause natural disasters and disease if provoked

We can see there are some words on the prayer flags when travelling in Tibet. It is not known whether the Bon believers ever wrote words on prayer flags. Even if no writing was added to the plain strips of cloth, it is likely that the Bon believers painted sacred symbols on them. Some symbols seen on Buddhist prayer flags today undoubtedly have Bonpo origins, their meaning now enhanced with the deep significance of Vajrayana Buddhist philosophy. Originally the words and images on prayer flags were painted by hand, one at a time. Woodblocks, carefully carved in mirror image relief, were introduced from China in the 15th century. This invention made it possible to reproduce identical prints of the same design. Traditional designs could then be easily passed down from generation to generation.

Nowadays, Tibetan people have a tradition of replacing prayer flags on Tibetan New Year, Saga Dawa Festival, etc. Tourists can make a Tibetan Festival Tour to experience such a tradition.

Tibetan Culture Heritage

Qinghai-Tibet Plateau has long been known as the sea of songs and dances. Tibetans have also been reputed as an excellent ethnic group good at singing and dancing. During Tibetan Festivals, you can encounter all the locals dancing and singing together, whether boys or girls, young or old, men or women. Circle-dance, a typical kind of Tibetan dances, prevails in Tibet Autonomous Region, which is named as Guozhuang Dance in Qamdo, Zhuoxie Dance in Lhasa and Shannan, Duixie Dance in Shigatse.

In addition, Tibetan Opera, Heroic Epic-King Gesar and Tibetan music also draw great attention of tourists at home and abroad.

Understanding the importance of Tibetan music

Music is one major aspect of a country's identity, of its past, and where it hopes to be on the future world stage. We have been to many countries and always had a small interest in local pop cultures, comparing the most listened tracks with the most revered local bands and artists. It is quite easy nowadays to differentiate the chart music from the traditional vibe, especially where we live in China. The spectrum is diverse, the language is the obvious main characteristic that defines its origin. But the uses of different instruments and the way they are played are what is most enjoyable about music around the world

Tibetan music needs to be explored in your lifetime. It is equally empowering as it is sinister, and cuts right to the emotional core. There is something very unique about it, even more so when you are actually in the vicinity of a Tibetan party or live show. There are, of course, different sounds when it comes to Tibetan styles of music, which you will find in this article.

Tibetan Pop Music

Tibet abides to current Asian pop culture very well and in no way is that a bad thing. They are well represented by their local bands and singers, such as Tsering Gyurmey, who has become one of the faces of modern sounds in Tibet. Songs celebrating Tibet's traditions and past movements are commonplace for Tsering, and is well known and publicized for his fantastic, strong vocals; something which Tibetans believe is because of the high altitude. Some Tibetan singers have even made a name for themselves in neighbouring China and Japan including Alan Dowa Dolma and Gao Yuan Hong. Their voices are as powerful as Tsering's, and fit the confines of Asian pop music extremely comfortably. However, there is plenty to learn from the more traditional Tibetan music, so let's look at some key components

What Types of Music Does Tibet Have?

It is easy to identify at least five types of music exclusive of mainstream pop music (mentioned above).

Sino-Mongolian Music

The first is something that resembles an opera. The songs are pleasant and jovial, usually resounding an old Buddhist provincial teaching and are very much a group effort. You will find that flutes and lutes combine with some percussion beats to create a soft aroma of music that is thought to resemble a constant communication link with the divine world, one that only "perfect beings" are able to compose. It is officially named Sino-Mongolian music and is heard in the streets during festivals and parties.

Liturgical Chanting

The second is totally different and much more sinister, yet has acted as a relaxing tool for many people around the world. Liturgical Chanting is unlike anything else you have heard, as it needs the efforts of a chant leader (someone who also trains monks in Tibet), therefore being very religiously influenced. The instruments and voices may be rhythmically independent of each other, or they may coincide and proceed together in an unstressed rhythm of equal pulses, which creates a long and whirring drone during the ensemble. It is truly compelling and should definitely be used to help with relaxation

Antiphonal Overlapping Singing
The third is somewhat recognizable to the western world as it is basically a harmony played out in choral fashion with two or more people. It can be compared to an acapella band but much more subtle and slow. Labelled Antiphonal Overlapping Singing, it sounds very melodic and can be enjoyed and remembered by those that listen, therefore being more accessible for onlookers to join in.

he Mystery Dance
The fourth is by far the most active as it is accompanied by dancing and eccentric movement. The Mystery Dance is saved for the New Year festivals in February and March, when Tibet becomes united to see out the old year and welcome in the New Year. The dance and rapid-fire beats are designed to identify and scare away the old year's demons in man and state, and start the New Year on a high. It is a party vibe, with off-beat percussion instruments, flutes, stringed

instruments and loud singing combined to create an amazing, hectic show and experience for those watching.

Tibetan Folk
The fifth type of music is very much the more modern of the styles, but the lyrics focus mainly on Tibetan everyday life. It is common to hear songs of agriculture, love and friendships, as well as old Tibetan ideals of peace and compassion. Classed as Tibetan Folk, the songs are played in band form with choruses and verses.

Instruments to Listen Out For

Typically, Tibetan street and folk music is in acoustic form with the use of the Tungna, a four-stringed carved piece of wood topped with Yak skin. If accompanied, there could be a wide array of different percussion instruments used, such as cymbals, bells and drums. The beat doesn't often change during one song so it is easy to follow along. Other often-used instruments include bamboo flutes, thigh bone flutes, shell trumpets and four-metre long Tongin horns. All can be seen on the roads around Lhasa and around the Potala Palace during the day. It is certainly worth walking around the city and listening to the many sounds that are produced.

Within the monk chants, only very bassy instruments are used to complement the low continuous chants, and occasionally put together with a touch of cymbal and flute. The idea is to keep the monks and their listeners, in a constant state of peace and meditation. It is seriously one of the most peaceful sounds in the world, and can go on for hours until it takes its natural diminuendo

The music you will hear in Tibet will change your very soul, if you let it. The magnificent positive effects it has for the mind and body are unrivalled, the surrounding atmosphere encapsulates colours and dance, and people become part of the rhythm. Whether you are visiting Tibet any time soon, you have already visited Tibet, or you simply want to know what to expect from Tibetan music on YouTube, the varying forms of song that comes from this ancient and sophisticated nation are more than enough to take your attention.

Take yourself away from the norm, and try the Tibetan vibes. We are big fans, especially of the Liturgical Chanting, so we would love to hear what you think!

Tibetan Opera

Tibetan Opera is called "Lhamo" or "Ace Lhamo" in Tibetan language, meaning "Sister Fairy". It employs songs, dances, chants and drama to tell stories, with most of its repertoire deriving from Buddhist teachings and Tibetan history. The folk opera is very popular in Tibet, especially in Lhasa, Lhokha, Shigatse and Chamdo, and also widespread in the nearby provinces like Sichuan, Gansu, Qinghai and Yunnan Provinces. Tibetan opera is also a hot option of entertainment for Tibet tours.

Compared with the few other folk operas of Chinese ethnic minorities, the Tibetan opera has the longest history. It dates back about 14 centuries. According to Tibetan historical records, King Songtsan Gambo greatly admired the costumes, music and dancing of the Tang Dynasty introduced to Tibet by Princess Wencheng of the Tang Dynasty when she married the Tibetan king. He arranged for the training of 16 beautiful girls in a combined art form of the Tang-style and Tibetan folk music and dancing in order to entertain the princess. Later, this entertainment developed into a more clearly defined form of dancing and singing.

Such performances gradually developed into Tibetan Opera and became very popular around Tibet. Since the 17th century, Tibetan Opera has had a rapid development and reached its peak with a long list of excellent players and traditional repertoires. Different genres evolved, each with a certain style. Performances were held during various festive occasions. The Shoton Festival which was once a religious festival became a special festive occasion of Tibetan Opera joint performance, during which many professional and amateur troupes were summoned to Lhasa to entertain the Dalai Lama and his followers.

Over the centuries, Tibetan opera has formed a three-part stage format. In the prelude, known as "Wenbadun," Wenba men in blue masks, two Jialu men and several fairies take the stage, performing religious rituals, and songs and dances. A narrator will expansively introduce the story, the characters and the libretto in rapid repetitive rhythm. The second part is the opera itself. All the players enter and start singing and dancing. The third part is an epilogue which features a blessing ceremony and is also an occasion for the presentation of hada(silk ritual greeting scarves) and donations from the audience. The highlight of the performance is its masks, through which the role of the players can be identified. The masks have various colors and motifs, each indicating a certain meaning. For example, the red mask refers to the king, the green the queen, while the yellow the lamas.

In the past, Tibetan Opera was only held outdoors, and each player only had one costume throughout the performance. Since the 1960s, Tibetan Opera has been performed indoors with lighting, backdrop, set, orchestral obbligato and a number of modern themes added. Today, changes have taken place in the structure, singing, dancing, masks and stage format of Tibetan opera, and an orchestra, backdrop, lighting and make-up have been added. Besides being performed in the open air, Tibetan operas are also performed on indoor stages. The stage format can be either traditional or modern. In the traditional format, a narrator explains the plot of the opera section by section as the opera is being performed episode.

Tibetan Opera is performed during important Tibetan Festivals, such as Tibetan New Year, Shoton Festival. The biggest Tibetan opera performances are held in Norbulingka Summer Palace during Shoton Festival in August

Tibetan Heroic Epic - King Gesar

King Gesar is a heroic epic created by the Tibetans from a collection of ancient legends, myths, verses, proverbs and various other folk cultures of Tibet. Originating via folk oral traditions, King Gesar was passed down from generation to generation orally in a combination of song and narration for over 1,000 years.

The Tibetan epic was formed between around 200 BC or 300 BC and 600 AD. In the later years, some folk balladeers continued to pass on the story orally; this enriched the plots and embellished the languages. The story had gradually become near perfect and very popular in the early 12th Century. The epic began to be compiled mainly by the monks of Nyingmapa (Red Sect of Tibetan Buddhism) in about the 11th Century, and were mainly hand-written books.

So far, King Gesar has been collected in more than 120 volumes, with more than one million verses (over 20 million words) — 25 times the length of the Western classic, Homer's Iliad. King Gesar, the greatest work of Tibetan literature, is easily the longest epic in the world, which has also appeared in ballads among the Mongols and Tus. The epic has been translated into languages of other brother nationalities of China as well as English, French, Russian, German, Indian and other foreign languages. It has now become a subject on study and is even discussed as a topic in the international seminar.

Gesar of Ling

In Tibetan-inhabited areas Gesar was known as the king of the ancient Tibetan kingdom of the Ling. The great hero and his brave army are kept alive in the rich, imaginative retellings of the epic. From early times, the epic was passed on orally. Today, a small number of inscribed woodblocks of the epic can be found in Lhasa, Xigaze and Dege County in Sichuan Province; a few handwritten copies are also dispersed among some families. The Potala Palace contains a statue of Gesar, which still attracts pilgrims on a daily basis. Gesar's deeds were recorded in the Kangba region more than anywhere else, and handwritten and printed versions of Gesar from Dege are considered the most authoritative works. People still argue that the village of Ngaxu in Northern Dege County was the birthplace of Gesar.

King Gesar Story

King Gesar of the Ling Kingdom was born in the 11th century as the son of the supreme god Indira. As a boy, he was very mischievous, but divine by nature and full of supernatural powers. His greatest enemy was his uncle -- a cowardly, vain and pretentious man who hoped to rule the country. Although the hero and his mother were banished, Gesar's exile enabled him to nurture his hidden strengths. He emerged victorious in a horse race to become king of the nation. King Gesar then began conquering the "kingdoms of demons" — the Jiang and Hor (northern Mongolian people) kingdoms. The war between the Ling and Hor kingdoms constituted one of the central parts of the story. It began with a beautiful girl, Qomu, who was King Gesar's queen. The Hor king, also known as the "White Tent King," heard about her beauty and sent for her. When his request was refused, he sent troops to attack the Ling kingdom. After several battles, another girl was sent to the Hor king in the place of Qomu. But once the truth was uncovered, the battles resumed. The Ling capital, along with Queen Qomu, was finally captured by Hor troops. But King Gesar organized all his troops with the help of an important Hor general, captured the Hor capital, killed the White Tent King and rescued his queen.

King Gesar Images

Gesar's image and story are immortalized in carvings, paintings, murals, woodcuts, embroideries, songs, dances and plays. Tibet has a research institute specializing in the study of the epic, whose research projects are listed as key State projects. Since 1979, the institute has collected more than 180 different song and narration versions of the epic, 55 woodblock and mimeographed editions and has recorded 70 performances of the epic on more than 3,000 recording tapes. Since liberation, China's related research institutes have been working on this monumental portion of world literature by gathering, sorting, collecting, studying and publishing the material on a large scale.

By the means of the integration of romanticism and realism, the epic tells the story how the hero, King Gesar, conquers all the devils and brings happiness to the people with his perseverance and magic strength. The epic also expresses the theme of the people's wish for justice and bliss. The background of the story spans from the three periods of ancient Tibet: Clanship in the late Prehistoric Times, the Slavery Period, and Serfdom in the Feudal Society. The epic is really an encyclopedia of the social and historical changes, relationships among classes and nationalities, ethnical cultures and customs of Tibet.

Plots of King Gesar - Tibetan Epic

The Tibetan heroic epic, King Gesar is set in the distant past, when the common Tibetan people were suffering from many natural disasters and vicious devils and living rather a miserable life. Demons and spirits ran wild. To deliver the people from their troubles, the merciful Avalokitesvara or Bodhisattva of Compassion, asked the Amitabha, the master of the western Pure Land, to dispatch a son of a heavenly deity, Toiba Gawa, who later came to be known as Gesar, to descend to the world and help the people. Since his birth, King Gesar had begun to exterminate the evils for Tibetans.

Gesar descended upon the earth and became king of the Tibetan people later. With his great abilities to defeat the demons and aid the poor and common people, Gesar was portrayed as a combination of god, dragon and a fierce spirit known as nyan in primitive Tibetan religion. He was endowed with special characteristics and marvelous powers and abilities, also suffering several trials. However, his invincible powers and protection from the God of Heaven helped him to survive and eventually defeat the demons.

Throughout his human life, Gesar labored to abolish the scourges that plagued the lives of the common people. At the age of five, he and his mother with a tribe 'Ling' moved to the banks of the Yellow River. When he was eight, they were joined by the members of the Ling tribe. At the age of 12, Gesar won a victory in a horseracing match and then became the leader of the tribe. Gesar then married Sengjam Zholmo and led expeditions against his enemies, defeating the northern demons that had invaded the Ling Kingdom.

In successive campaigns, Gesar defeated King Gurdkar of the Hor Kingdom, King Sadam of the Jiang Kingdom, King Shingkhri of Monyul, King Nor of Tangzig, King Chidan of Khachevigyu, King Toigui of the Zugu Kingdom and scores of other small tribes and minor kingdoms known as zongs in ancient Tibet. After he finished his glorious missions, King Gesar took his mother and his beautiful empress back to heaven, bringing the grand epic of his life to a dramatic close

Guozhuang Dance - Tibetan Dance

Guozhuang means singing and dancing in a circle, homophonic with Guoxie in Tibetan language. It originated from the form by which Tibetans danced around a campfire, all the time. This dance has been with the Tibetan ethnic group throughout their history.

There are three kinds of Guozhuang: Temple Guozhuang, Farm Guozhuang and Pastoral Guozhuang.

The Temple Guozhuang event is organized for religious purposes in temples or monasteries, or for greeting and sending-off the Living Buddha. It is solemn with strong religious implications, through which believers dance in honor of the Living Buddha, grateful for their expected bliss in their afterlife.

The Farm Guozhuang consists of two parts: singing, and quick singing and dancing. The tempo is subdivided into slow, medium and quick. At the beginning of a performance men and women stand in two separate circles and sing in rotation while swaying and stamping their feet. They conclude their singing by shouting "Ya!" Then their steps quicken and come to a stop at an exuberant allegro. The allegro music is often a condensed version of the slow music. The Farm Guozhuang is popular in Qamdo in eastern Tibet, while the Pastoral Guozhuang is popular in the vast pasture land of Damxung, Heihe and Sog Xian.

The form of pastoral Guozhuang is largely the same as farm Guozhuang, but there is a big difference in movement. In pastoral Guozhuang, for instance, the dancers jump while waving their hands in front of their chests and step forward, and then turn left or right, and their hands and feet move in the same direction. The sonorous singing produces a magnificent effect.

The movements of Guozhuang are agile and vigorous. The loose, wide trousers of the male dancers look like the feathered legs of eagles, and the men's movements are imitative of creatures, especially eagles, such as an eagle spreading its wings, hopping, and soaring. Women expose their right arms during dancing, with the right sleeve waggling behind. Moving around a circle, they sway their joined hands frontward and backward, keeping beats of their steps, until very late at night.

The emphasis is on the postures and expression of emotion. The verses for one song read: "Oh snow-capped mountains, make way for us. We fly with wings spread. Oh rivers, make way for us. We stride with broad steps." These old verses display Tibetans' brave and bold character.

Zhuoxie Dance

Zhuoxie is a kind of public dance with a long-handle oval drum tied to one's waist, popular in Lhasa and rural Shannan areas. While dancing, the drummer will beat the drum with two curved drumsticks. Zhuoxie means song and dance in Tibetan language.

Zhuoxie consists mainly of three parts. The first part is entirely dance. Its slow tempo gradually quickens. The people dance to the drumbeat in changing patterns to express their feelings. Sometimes a special display of skill in beating the drums is given. The drum teams in Nedong County are known for their vigorous beating while shaking their heads. The second part is singing. Holding tall feathers, the troupe, in a semicircle facing the audience, sing songs to express their wishes for a happy occasion. In the third part the performers beat the drums while singing. They conclude the performance with a bow to the audience.

Zhuoxie dance has always been performed at ceremonies of blessing and for entertaining guests. The villages of Nedong, Zalang, Qonggya and Sagya in Shannan region all have waist drum teams of their own. Most of them perform the drum dance. Even numbers of people participate in the dance for the convenience of changing patterns. The leader of the dance, zhuoben, wearing sheepskin and a mask, appears first. Holding tata (coloured arrows), he stands in the centre to conduct the dance and drumbeat. Sometimes he shouts out the drumbeat, "One beat, three beats, five beats, seven beats, nine beats," to coordinate the drumming and dancing.

Zhuoxie does not use any special musical instruments for accompaniment except for small bells fastened to the performers' knees. One version of Zhuoxie depicts the construction of Sagya

Monastery: clearing the ground, driving piles, transporting bricks and building with rocks, praying to god for protection, a lion playing with a tiger, setting the pillars and roof beams in place, fixing doors and windows, clearing the dust, welcoming the king to ascend the throne, imitating a walking crow, weaving carpets, and inauguration of the structure to express best wishes to the people.

Zhuoxie became popular in Yalong and the rest parts of Tibet in the 17th century, not only was it performed in the inauguration ceremony for the Sangye temple and recorded but also performed again on the magnificent and glorious wedding ceremony when the Tibet king Songtsen gampo married the princess Wencheng from the Tang empire according to some legends. For more than one thousand years, the dance Zhuoxie has been showing its lasting vitality.

Large-Scale Tibetan Natural Lyrics : Happiness on the Way

"Approaching Tibet, you are approaching harmony and happiness. Leaving Tibet, you take happiness with you on the way. Recalling Tibet above the bright clouds. The long way to happiness stretches far beyond, and the eulogy song for happiness flies forever. The faith in the pursuit of happiness is burning for happiness is right on the way". The following is pictures of the "Large-scale Tibetan Natural Lyrics:

Happiness on the Way" performed by the tibetans during the 2008 Olympic Games in Beijing

Duixie Dance - Tibetan Tap Dance

Duixie is a popular folk dance in rural areas of western Tibet. In Tibetan language, Dui means "upper" or "highland", referring to the round dance popular in rural areas of Ngamring, Dingri, Lhatse, and Sagya counties at Shigatse Prefecture on the upper reaches of the Yarlung Zangbo River, while Xie means "songs." Therefore, Duixie actually means a performance by dancing and singing

Duixie also refers to the tap dance performed by urban people after the folk dances was introduced into Lhasa. It becomes a cheerful and enthusiastic folk dance popular throughout Tibet, and later, after improvement by actors and dancers, evolved into a kind of urbanized Tibetan tap dance. Most popular on the streets and in the open squares and Lingkas (parks) in Lhasa, this dance is also known as the Lhasa Tap Dance.

The popular tap dance that has evolved from the rural Duixie Dance is a complex combination of a change of movement after every three steps — five, seven, and nine quick mark-time steps with turns. The taps are rhythmic.

In the mid-seventeenth century the fifth Dalai, in an effort to reinforce his rule by combining government with religion, stipulated that Shoton Festival be held in Lhasa from the end of June to early July every year. During the Shoton Festival, groups from all parts of Tibet converged on Lhasa to perform. A group from a dui area in Tibet performed a lively and vigorous tap dance that was immediately loved and improved on by people in Lhasa. The major improvement was to start on the second beat, followed by a change of step after every three steps.

In Duixie Dance, the dancers tap vigorously to music played on flutes, Chinese plucked stringed instruments, plucked six-stringed instruments, dulcimers and clusters of small bells. The music for accompaniment of Duixie has been formalized into a slow opening, short interlude, allegro and finale. This Duixie has gradually been transformed from a recreational dance to stage exhibition.

Tibetan Arts

Tibetan arts originated from the rock paintings in ancient time and its contents ranged from animal images of deer, ox, sheep, horse, etc to hunting scenes. Tibetan arts have developed very well during the period of Tubo Kingdom. Especially after introducing Buddhism to Tibet, religious paintings made a further progress. The heritage of traditional Tibetan crafts and the fusion of India, Nepal and Han People's art essence make Tibetan arts outstand in the world. Tourists can get a panorama view of Tibet arts through stone and rock carvings, murals, frescos, sand mandala and precious Thangkas.

As a kind of folk art, Tibetan carving is Tibetan culture in miniature. It records the past days of Tibetan area and people's life. The contents in stone and rock carvings have covered Tibetan daily necessities, fairy gods, Bon religion, folk legend, historical figures and Tibetan Buddhism, etc. Three typical representatives of Tibetan rock carvings are really worth your visit, namely, Ritu Rock Carving in Ngari,

Yaowangshan Rock Carving in Lhasa and Zaxi Cave Rock Carving in Nagqu.

Tibetan murals and frescos are the actual pictures of Tibetan history, from which you can find the trace of Tibetan politics, economy, culture, customs and medicine. And it also has abundant subjects, including Buddhist teachings, fairy tales, local lives, natural scenery, etc. The best place to appreciate Tibetan murals are Potala Palace, Jokhang Temple, and Ruins of Guge Kingdom.

Different from oil painting and frescos, Tibetan Thangkas are often painted on cloth, silk, brocade and paper. Most of them focus on Tibetan religions, depicting the life of Buddha and historical stories of important Lamas. While joining Buddha Exhibition Festival in Tashilhunpo Monastery, you'll recognize how important Thangka it is to local Tibetans.

Tibetan Thangka Paintings

Anyone visiting Tibet and exploring its culture should visit the temples and monasteries to view the vibrant and educational Tibetan Thangka paintings. Painted by hand on cloths of silk or cotton, these bright, colorful paintings usually depict a Buddhist deity or other religious scene. When they are not in use, they remain rolled up like scrolls, with coverings on the back and front to protect the painting. Kept this way, the Thangkas can last for a very long time, but are affected by moisture, so need to be kept in a very dry place.

Traditionally, the Thangka are designed to tell the life of Buddha, as well as other influential lamas and deities. The Tibetan word THANG KA means "recorded message" in English. The composition of the Thangka is very complex and elaborate, and often incorporates the central figure - normally a deity - surrounded by many smaller figures, in a symmetrical design. Although they are less common, narrative scenes are also depicted on Thangkas. Thangka are also used as devotional pieces during religious rituals or ceremonies, and can be used as a medium for prayer. Moreover, Thangkas can aid in the spiritual path to enlightenment as the religious art is used as a meditation tool. Devotees often have Thangka paintings hung in their homes, bedrooms and offices.

Overview of Tibetan Culture and Arts

In Tibet, you will always be amazed by the artistic wonders: the architectures, the prayer-flags, sculptures and Thangkas, songs and dances, which are representation of the Tibetan cultures. Tibetan arts have gone through a 5000 years of history. The prehistoric art was closely bound up with the aboriginal Bon religion, while its later development relied greatly on the Tibetan Buddhist culture. Therefore, it has been imbued with strong ethnic and regional features.

Bon is the main aboriginal religion during the prehistoric civilization on Qinghai-Tibetan Plateau, which was established in the 5th century B.C. by Shenrab Miwoche, the prince of Zhang-zhung kingdom in western Tibet. Around the first century A.D. the religion began to spread eastward until fully distributed in Tsang region and Lhasa region. This marked its first zenith when it almost dominated the political, economic and cultural life in the early stage of the Tubo Kingdom. Bon advocated pantheism and believed that "every thing has a soul". The deities, the supernatural powers of mountains, rivers, lakes, seas, the sun, the moon, stars, wind, rain, thunder, lightening, birds, and beast, etc. as many as one can enumerate, govern the birth, ageing, sickness, death, events and fortune of people, who could not predict and control their own destinies because people are believed to be created by the deities.

In the 7th century A.D., Buddhism was introduced to Tubo Kingdom on a large scale and Bon lost its dominance in the mid 8th century. Tibetan Buddihism has been ramified into four major sects: Nyingma

Sect, Kadam Sect, Sakya Sect, Kagyu Sect and Gulug up to the 15th century. These sects had later on brought significant and extensive impacts on political, economic and cultural life of Tibetan people in progression of different period of time.

The Tibetan arts have been inevitably dyed with a distinctive religious arts, especially the Tibetan Buddhist ones, have constituted the main body of the Tibetan arts and made it stand out in utterly different way among the others.

Buddha is the sovereign of the realm of Tibetan Buddhism, and is the most frequently occurred figure in Tibetan art works as well. The major subject matters of Tibetan arts include Buddha, Bodhisattvas and a Variety of Deities, the mandala, the Gurus and Dharma Kings, the biographic Stories and Jataka Stories of Sakyamuni.

The major art forms are composed of Tibetan Architectures including Ancient Tomb Architectures, Monastery Architectures, Palace Architectures, Tibetan Residence Architectures; Tibetan Sculptures including Buddhist Sculptures, Metal Sculptures, Clay Modelings, Stone Carvings, Tibetan Paintings including Thangka, fresco, rock drawing and contemporary painting; Tibetan Handicrafts, Metal

Wares, Masks, Block-Printing, Textiles Handicrafts and Wooden Wares.

The Origins of the Thangka

The Tibetan Thangka is an art form that originated in Nepal, and was brought to Tibet by Nepalese princess, Bhrikuti, who was the wife of Songtsen Gampo, the founder of the Tibetan Empire. The paintings were developed over the centuries from the early wall murals that can be seen in a few remaining sites like the Ajanta Caves in India and the Mogao Caves in Gansu Province, China. The Mogao Caves have extensive wall paintings, and were previously a repository for many Tibetan paintings on cloth, which are some of the earliest surviving Thangka, as well as other manuscripts, paintings and prints. The earliest dated prints from the "Library Cave" were dated to be from around 780-848 AD, when the region was under Tibetan rule.

Thangka form was developed alongside the more traditional wall paintings of the Tibetan Buddhists, which were mostly found in monasteries and temples. Many of the early Thangka were commissioned by rich individuals who believed they would gain merit for doing so. Many notable monks also had their own Thangka, as personal meditation images, and would have an inscription on the back. Many of the older Thangka in Tibet now are from the 11th and

12th centuries, and were already complex in their design. However, the backgrounds would be mostly sky with a little landscape. The Thangka continued to develop in style and complexity over the following centuries, with the different monastic orders developing slightly different characteristics and styles.

Types of Thangka in Tibet

Traditional Thangkas come in a variety of types, based on the different techniques and materials used. They are generally divided into two rather broad categories: painted Thangka and appliqué, or embroidered Thangka. They are then further divided into another seven sub-categories which are:

1. Painted in color, which are the most common type
2. Appliqué, an ornamental needlework made from pieces of fabric
3. Black Background, which uses a gold line on a black background
4. Block-prints, the paper or cloth outlined renderings, made by woodblock printing
5. Embroidery with multicolored threads
6. Gold Background, a very auspicious treatment which was used for peaceful deities and the fully enlightened Buddhas
7. Red Background, this was also a gold line, but on vermilion pigmented cloth

Thangkas are traditionally painted on either cotton or silk, with a loosely woven cotton being the most common. They are normally around 40cm-58cm wide, and the larger ones frequently have a seam in the support. The paints are made from pigments in a water-soluble form of animal glue. The pigments used come from both mineral and organic sources, and were mixed warm and applied almost immediately to the painting.

Thangka Composition

The paintings are composed in the way of most Buddhist art, being highly geometric and symmetrical in form. All of the composite parts of the Thangka are laid out in a grid of intersecting lines and angles, and the artists would have a set of pre-designed "templates" to work from, ranging from the alms bowls of the Buddha to the size, shape and angles of the individual facial features.

As Thangka are explicitly religious paintings, they must be laid out following strict guidelines that the artists are trained in. Artists must also have a good religious understanding, background and knowledge in order to create an appropriately accurate Thangka. Everything from the color to the proportions to the position of the hands is laid out in the rules to correctly personify the Buddha and Deities.

Tibetan Festivals and Thangka Display

Thangka is so much a part of Tibetan culture that there are dedicated Thangka Unveiling Festivals that showcase this unique art, as well as Thangka being shown at many other festivals throughout the year. At Tashilunpo Monastery, the monks unveil the big Thangka with an image of Buddha and the people will all gather in front of it to pray.

In August, the Ganden Thangka Festival, held at the old Ganden Monastery, there are thousands of people who walk a kora around the monastery before going inside to pray. Then they will all gather outside to view and pray before the woven image of Buddha. On this festive occasion, pilgrims dress in their finest clothes, and move from temple to temple with offerings and hoping to receive blessings from the monks. The Thangka that is displayed here is normally around 200 feet wide and 150 feet tall, and causes an uproar of the crowd as it is unveiled

And at the Shoton Festival, one of the most popular of Tibet's traditional festivals, the Thangka is unveiled at the Drepung Monastery in Lhasa. As the sound of the horn echoes through the valley, a host of lamas carry the huge portrait of Qamba Buddha from the Coqen Hall and towards the western end of the monastery to a specially erected platform. As smoke rises from all sides and monks chant scriptures, the lamas slowly unroll the Thangka to cheers from the crowds, who rush to the painting to offer their white hada, or prayer silks. This Thangka is only open for around two hours, before the monks move it carefully back inside for another yea

Where to Buy Thangka Painting for Souvenir

Most Thangkas are small in comparison to a traditional western portrait, but those used for displays can be several meters long, and can be seen at many of the Tibetan Thangka festivals. For those who wish to have a Thangka of their own, they only need to pay a visit to Lhasa's Barkhor Street. Part of the kora around the Jokhang Temple, the street is full of things for sale, from Tibetan rugs and crafts to broadswords and Thangka. You can easily bargain with the sellers, as this is almost traditional, and you can get your souvenirs for a very good price. And don't forget to circumambulate the kora clockwise, as the other pilgrims do.

There is also a Thangka painting store on East Barkhor Street, where you can buy this beautiful Tibetan artwork, and learn more about the art and history of the Tibetan Thangka.

Thangka are a beautiful and very spiritual part of Buddhism, and a huge part of the rich Tibetan culture. It is easy to see why these paintings are so popular, and how the art has survived in the region for centuries.

Sand Mandala in Tibet and Its Profound Philosophy

Tibet is known for its colourful artwork involving Buddhist deities, Buddha figures and aspects of Buddhist philosophy. Anyone who is even remotely familiar with Tibetan culture will be familiar with one particular type of artwork- the Sand Mandala. A mandala is basically a spiritual symbol depicting the universe and the cosmos. It is generally a geometric pattern which represents the universe metaphorically

Mandalas are very common in Tibetan culture where they represent various philosophies found in Tibetan Buddhism like the structure of the Universe, Wisdom and Impermanence, Nature of Enlightenment, etc. Tibetan Mandalas are always made using coloured sand hence the name the Sand Mandala. For a traveller visiting Tibet for the first time, understanding the significance and philosophy of Sand Mandalas will make the experience of seeing one in reality a profound one.

Artistic and Philosophical Carrier of Tibetan Buddhism

Sand Mandalas or Dul-Tson-Kyil-Khor (Mandala of coloured powders) as they are known in Tibetan, is an ancient art form of Tibetan

Buddhism. Tibetan Buddhism has many colourful art forms like painting Thangkas, Butter sculptures and Sand Mandalas. Like all the other art forms of Tibet, the sand mandala is associated with Buddhist culture and Buddhist philosophy.

Making of Sand Mandala

Sand Mandalas have been in the Tibetan art culture for centuries. In the olden days, monks would use precious and semi-precious stones in place of coloured sand. Nowadays using gemstones is not practical so monks use dyed sand. The sand in usually very dense so it doesn't easily scatter if there is a wind or some disturbance while the mandala is being made

First the monks draw the basic design of the mandala on a flat board. Then they start filling in the outline with the coloured sand. Usually they start at the centre and work outwards. Creating a mandala involves a lot of cooperation and the aim is to maintain harmony throughout the entire process. Completion of a mandala can take several weeks, which is why it is a group effort by the monks. It is generally a very meditative process for monks due to the intense concentration involved.

The mandala starts with a dot in the centre which represents the primary deity of the mandala. At this dot, the image of the deity is drawn. Work on the mandala is started first by holding a few ceremonies. Outsiders are rarely permitted to view the beginning ceremonies, which involve dancing, chanting and prayers. Once these ceremonies are over, work on the mandala begins.

The sand mandalas are done by skilled professionals, who are always monks. These monks are trained in this art form for many years before they are allowed to create them in public. They are trained in the very specific rules of mandala design and its philosophy. Training can go to more than three years. Mandalas are created using the rules given out in various Tibetan esoteric texts. There are specific rules for different types of mandalas.

Each mandala will vary in its colour, shape, size and design depending on the lesson it aims to teach. Creating a mandala involves enormous patience, perseverance and willpower. It is a painstaking work that produces breathtaking results at the end. What is even more awesome is that after all this work is finished and the traditional ceremonies associated with it are over, the mandala is destroyed by being swept aside. The significance of this will be explained further in this article.

Philosophical Significance of Sand Mandala

The mandala is steeped in symbolism and philosophy. Before a monk ever makes any mandala, he is first educated in the philosophy behind it. Since a mandala is so rich in symbolism, the very act of creating the mandala is believed to be sacred. On the whole a mandala usually represents the universe. It can also represent various other things like the Enlightened mind, Wisdom and Impermanence, etc

Generally a mandala is represented in the form of a palace. In the middle of the mandala palace is where the Buddha essence lies. Surrounding him are the four "gates", which form a square. They in turn represent the four directions as well as the four immeasurables of Buddhism, which are loving-kindness, compassion, altruistic joy and equanimity.

In each of the directions is a Buddha called a Dhyani Buddha. While these Buddhas are usually the same colour, they can be distinguished by their hand gestures. They each represent overcoming a particular defilement like ignorance or anger or lust. Outside this are generally concentric circles which also have deep meanings. The outermost ring is usually drawn as a ring of fire. This denotes the burning of ignorance. The mandala is technically a representation of the enlightened mind. So an outer circle showing a ring of fire means the first step towards enlightenment would be the burning away of ignorance. It also symbolizes the transformations that humans must go through to reach enlightenment.

The next circle is depicted by thunderbolts and diamond scepters. This is linked to the Tibetan tradition itself which is called Vajrayana or Diamond Vehicle Buddhism. It represents illuminity and indestructibility of the the ultimate truth of the Buddha's teachings

The inner two layers depict eight graveyards and finally lotus leaves. These represent the eight aspects of human consciousness that bind a person to the cycle of rebirth and religious rebirth, respectively. After that is the square "palace", the meaning of which has been discussed earlier.

The mandala represents the human journey from ignorance to Buddhahood. One interesting thing about the process of mandala making is that, after the mandala is completed, the accompanying ceremonies and public viewing is over, the mandala is destroyed in one swift sweep. This represents the ultimate impermanence of all conditioned things. The sand is then swept into the rivers where it is believed that the river waters will carry the blessed sand far and wide.

Mandala making is very important in Tibetan Buddhism and it is heavily laden with symbolism and deep philosophy. Sand mandalas are beautiful, colourful and a definite treat to the eyes of those seeing them.

Tibetan Thangka Art

Tibetan Thangka

Tibetan Thangka is a Nepalese art form exported to Tibet after Princess Bhrikuti of Nepal, a daughter of King Lichchavi and a wife of Sron Tsan Gampo. Generally, a Thangka is a Tibetan silk painting with embroidery, usually depicting a Buddhist deity, famous scene, or mandala of some sort. It is sometimes called a scroll-painting. There is also woodcarving basso-relievo Thangka.

Unlike an oil painting or acrylic painting, the thankga is not a flat creation, but consists of a painted or embroidered picture panel, over which a textile is mounted, and then over which is laid a cover, usually silk. Generally, thankgas last a very long time and retain much of their lustre, but because of their delicate nature, they have to be kept in dry places so as to prevent the quality of the silk from being affected by moisture.

The Tibetan Thangka, when created properly, perform several different functions. Originally, thangka painting became popular among traveling monks because the scroll paintings were easily rolled and transported from monastery to monastery. Images of deities can be used as important teaching tools when depicting the life (or lives) of the Buddha, describing historical events concerning important Lamas, or retelling myths associated with other deities and bodhisattvas. One popular subject is

The Wheel of Life, which is a visual representation of the Abhidharma teachings (Art of Enlightenment). Devotional images act as the centerpiece during a ritual or ceremony and are often used as mediums through which one can offer prayers or make requests. Overall, and perhaps most importantly, religious art is used as a meditation tool to help bring one further down the path to enlightenment. The Buddhist Vajrayana practitioner uses a thanga image of their yidam, or meditation deity, as a guide, by visualizing "themselves as being that deity, thereby internalizing the Buddha qualities (Lipton, Ragnubs)."

To Buddhists these Tibetan religious paintings offer a beautiful manifestation of the divine, being both visually and mentally stimulating.

Historians note that Chinese painting had a profound influence on Tibetan painting in general. Starting from the 14th and 15th century, Tibetan painting had incorporated many elements from the Chinese, and during the 18th century, Chinese painting had a deep and far-stretched impact on Tibetan visual art. According to Giuseppe Tucci, by the time of the Qing Dynasty, "a new Tibetan art was then developed, which in a certain sense was a provincial echo of the Chinese 18th century's smooth ornate preciosity."

As an important Tibetan painting form, Thangka with a huge variety of styles, involves mastery of many demanding techniques: mastery in sketching the illustrations and numerous deities according to formal iconography rules laid down by generations of Tibetan masters; learning to grind and apply the paints, which are made from natural stone pigments; and learning to prepare and apply details in pure gold. From the canvas preparation and drawing of the subject, through to mixing and applying colors, decorating with gold, and mounting the finished work in brocade, the creation of a thangka painting involves skill and care at each stage and displays meticulous detail and exquisite artisanship.

Therefore, the process of learning to paint thangkas is rigorous. In the first three years, students learn to sketch the Tibetan Buddhist deities using precise grids dictated by scripture. The two years following are devoted to the techniques of grinding and applying the mineral colors and pure gold used in the paintings. In the sixth year, students study in detail the religious texts and scriptures used for the subject matter of their work. To become an accomplished thangka painter, at least ten years training is required under the constant supervision of a master. After the training process, students still need five to ten years to become experts in the field. Most importantly, Tibetan Thangka painting requires extended concentration, attention to detail, and knowledge of Buddhist philosophy, and must be carried out in a peaceful environment.

Qamo Dance - Tibetan Religious Dance

Qamo, a Tibetan religious dance related to Tibetan Buddhism, is a well-established performance art form combining scripture-chanting in perfect unison with music and dance. Qamo dance is usually performed in temples by monks with solemn and splendid atmospheres so as to subdue evil spirits in monasteries.

The religious dance Qamo in Tibet came into being during the conflict between Buddhism and the aboriginal Bon religion. In the process of localizing Buddhism, Padmasambhava from Kashmir created a kind of religious dance to subdue the "evil spirits" in monasteries by giving the local Tibetan dances Buddhist interpretations. This religious dance gradually became popular as Qamo, a sorcerer's dance

According to Chronicles of Tibetan Kings, various kinds of animal-mime dances, divine-instrument dances, drum dances and flower-offering ceremonial dances appeared during the reign of Songzan Gambo in the seventh century.

Instead of absorbing the local Tibetan dances completely, Padmasambhava selected only some animal-mime dances and divine instrument dances that suited Buddhism and combined them with the ceremonial mask dance of the Bon-po religion. These dances and Ox Dance, Deer God Dance and Dharma Protector Dance, preserved to this day, trace back to the same origin.

Before the modern Sorcerer's Dance begins formally, a traditional livestock sacrificial ceremony is held. However, livestock is no longer killed since it goes against the doctrines of Buddhism. Mostly drawings are substituted.

When the ceremony begins, suona horns are blown and drums and cymbals beaten, a group of performers playing demons walk slowly round as a prelude to the dance. This is followed by the Demons' Dance, Skeleton Dance, Ox God Dance, Deer Dance, Guardian Dance and Dharma Protector Dance.

Between dances Lamas put on wrestling and acrobatic bouts to entertain the spectators. Sometimes, they perform stories from Buddhist scripture that bear messages to do good things in other people's interest, such as "Sacrifice Life to Save the Tiger" and "Dance of the Man of Longevity," who is believed to be generous in bestowing longevity and good fortune.

The last act is for the divine soldiers to drive away the evil spirits. With guns on their shoulders, the performers send Duoma (the leading demon, made of butter and tsampa) to the wilderness and burn him to drive away evil for the year and pray for good fortune in the coming year.

Tibetan Stone and Rock Carvings

Tibetan Stone and Rock Carvings

Tibet is in rich repositories of culturally significant stone and rock carvings. When you are travelling in Tibet, you will find stone and rock carvings everywhere. With diligence and wisdom, like their ancestors, Tibetans left excellent records of development and social changes on the Tibetan Plateau. These are being discovered and becoming widely known, as is their unique geographic environment and the unique ethnic culture that produced them.

Tibetan Rock Carving

Tibetan Rock Carving is a term to describe the line carvings and sculpted reliefs. Contents in Tibetan rock carvings are various including the solo patterns of animals, human figures, fairy gods, plants, utensils, architectures, signs and other natural articles. There are more than 80% rock carvings mainly describe animal images, so animals may be a typical character of Tibetan rock carvings. Rock carvings usually describe the hunting scenes and the daily life of the nomadic people. While some of them are related to the agriculture, for example, the plants and the star and moon images express the pray ceremony situation. Tibetan rock carvings are a historical book to record the past days of Tibetan people and the ancient ethnic groups. This artwork is an artistic language of the original troupes in Tibet. When the footprint of the past days is buried by the time, these Tibetan rock carvings provide valuable materials for us to dig more things about the original culture of Tibet.

Ritu Rock Carving, Yaowangshan Rock Carving and Zaxi Cave Rock Carving are three outstanding representatives of Tibetan Rock Carvings. Ritu Rock Carvings exist in the Ngari area. In these hundreds of rock carvings, contents include hunting activities, war and fighting, religious ceremonies, dancing scenes, etc. The major color tone of Ritu Rock Carving is red. The typical character of Ritu Rock Carvings is the simple composition drawn by simple techniques. Yaoshanwang Rock Carvings exist in the Yaowangshan Mountain in Lhasa. This kind of rock carvings is made in the modern time. The main articles in these carvings are religious figures. Zaxi Cave Rock Carvings are in the east bank of the Namtso Lake in Nagqu area. These carvings are spread in the 8 natural caves. Most of the carvings are colored in red. Patterns of this kind of carvings are animals, human, sun and pagodas, etc.

Tibetan Stone Carving

Black Stone Carvings

In Tibet, black stone can be found in ordinary Tibetan homes because it is seen as the propitious stone by Tibetan people who can drive the evil and befall the fortune. The stone carving is not very expensive because it is carved by machine not handcraft work.

Mani Stone Carving

Among the various kinds of Tibetan folk carvings, the most popular is Mani stone carving due to its vast subject matter and rich contents which have a unique Tibetan hue.

In Tibet, stone carvings are almost entirely related to religion; "Mani Pile," also known as "lection stone" plays an important part in forming this strong religious atmosphere. The "Mani pile" is a ubiquitous sight near villages or on Tibetan roadsides. Tibetan Buddhists place small rocks into piles, where each rock is inscribed with the six-word mystic teaching of truth (Om-ma-ni, pad-me-Hum) -- literally "Om! The jewel is in the lotus". A Tibetan will pause at a Mani pile to pray by walking around it clockwise. The subjects of Mani stone carvings are usually lections, Buddhas or Bodhisattvas. According to a carver, the lections or Buddhas on the stone are carved at the request of the relatives of the dead people to release souls from purgatory. Usually, the contents are decided by a Shaman.

Mani stone carving differs significantly from place to place in Tibet according to the demand, interest and materials. Mani stone carvings in western Tibet take on an elegant flavor, while those in eastern Tibet have an air of antiquity.

Despite natural erosion and the trials and tribulations of history, large numbers of Tibetan stone and rock carving artworks still survive today for people to view and study of various "Culture" series in the present day.

Tibetan stone carving culture broadly encompasses four periods: prehistory, slavery, feudal and socialism, reflecting the different nature of these societies. The content and expression of stone carving culture in various times corresponds to social patterns and represents Tibetan social development in different periods. This demonstrates that culture is affected and determined by the society that produces it.

Tibetan murals - Tibet painting art

Tibetan murals - Tibet painting art

Tibetan painting originated from rock painting in ancient times. Tibetan murals are evolved from early rock paintings consisting mainly of the animal images of deer, ox, sheep, horses, and hunting scenes. Rock painting was quite developed in ancient times, especially after Buddhism arrived, and religious painting was further developed.

Tibetan murals are lightly imbued with the essence of Tibet's indigenous religion, Bon. They also incorporate features from the religious and artistic traditions of India and Nepal, and each mural has its own unique characteristics. In each, a religious figure, animal or simple symbol, is featured with some appointed motifs. While the majority of the murals center on religious aspects of Tibetan culture, others portray historical figures or social activities. As many of these murals are religious in nature, murals are concentrated in temples, the holiest sites in Tibet, although they may be seen anywhere.

Tibetan murals contain rich content, involving religion, politics, history, economy, culture, Tibetan medicine, and social life. Any of the Buddhist scriptures, Buddhist messages, fairy tales, history stories, daily living scenes, mountains and rivers, birds and flowers, patterns and adornment can be adopted into a wall painting, which has a unique style. It uses cold and dark colors, such as black, dark blue, mauve, dark grey, brown and white; drawing with lines, especially plain lines; simple, rough and sparse outlines. It has the same style of art as the atmosphere of the monastery, and contains exaggerated and distorted art images.

Brightly colored wall paintings can be found everywhere in Tibetan monasteries. Some of them are more than 1300 years old. As it is recorded in Tibetan history, in the year when Songtsen Gampo, the Tibetan king, inherited the throne, it is said he saw Sakyamuni, Horse-necked Diamond King, Tara, Stationary Vajrapani, and the four Buddhas. He told the Nepali artisan, Ciba, to carve the four Buddhas into a rock wall and paint them. This is the earliest wall painting and sculpture.

Tibetan mural experienced two periods. The first period starts after Songtsen Gampo became the king. Because he married a Khridzun princess of Nepal, and a Wenchen princess of the Tang Dynasty who brought Buddhist statues and Buddhist scriptures, he built Jokhang Monastery and Romoche Monastery, which affected the development of wall painting. The figures in the wall paintings of that period are chubby, and painted with simple color, which is close to the art works at Dunhuang by Bei Wei and the beginning of the Tang Dynasty. The second period started around 10 century A.C. when the initiator of the

Yellow sect, Zongkapa, reformed the religion. Yellow sects grew rapidly as the predominant religion. The number of yellow sect monasteries increased to 3000. During that period, the political and religious leaders collected many folk painters to complete wall painting jobs, and let them run in the families. That is the most splendid period of wall painting.

The painters gave human life to the statue of Buddha through art, which make the statue look faithful, handsome, merciful, charming, fiery and forthright. Such works exist as picture-story book in all the monasteries. Each of these images has distinct features that can be easily recognized by someone who knows a little bit of Tibetan culture.

Tibetan wall painting is actually pictures of Tibetan history. It describes visually social living, the development of religion, historical tales, local conditions and the customs of Tibet. Therefore, Tibetan murals can be classified as religious murals, historical murals, social murals, etc.

Religious Murals

Murals in Tibet focus primarily on religion. Although some early murals devoted to Bon still exist, most of the contemporary murals depict various aspects of Buddhism. The most popular murals are of religious figures, such as Buddhas, Bodhisattvas, Guardians of Buddhist Doctrines, Taras in the sutras, or Buddhist masters. In these paintings, there is always a head deity or human, who is usually surrounded by some other deities or humans. If the central figure is featured alone, his surroundings are extravagantly detailed. Jokhang Temple and Tashilhunpo Monastery have built special courtyards dedicated to this type of mural painting.

In addition to the murals of religious figures, there are also some that focus on religious activities, such as debating sutras, Changmo Dance, the Buddhist cosmologic mandalas , and other Buddhist morality tales. In certain temples, chains of pictures illustrate Tibetan legends or follow the lives of religious figures like Sakyamuni, the founder of Buddhism. One of the most famous legends about the Tibetan ancestors - a monkey and a Raksasi - is told in the murals of Potala Palace and Norbulingka.

Historical Murals

Based on the history of Tibet, these murals depict key historical figures and events. There are paintings of ancient Tibetan kings, like Songtsen Gampo (617-650), Trisong Detsen (742-798) and Tri Ralpa Chen (866-896) of Tubo Kingdom, as well as their famous concubines, Princess Wencheng and Princess Jincheng of Tang Dynasty (618-907) and Princess Bhrikuti of Nepal. Their stories are told through the series of pictures in Potala, Jokhang and Norbulingka.

In Potala, there are also chains of pictures about the biography of the 5th Dalai Lama , who had done much to facilitate the friendship of Tibet and the Chinese central government. Two other historical murals of note: in Ruins of Guge Kingdom there are a series of murals about the rise and down of Tubo Kingdom; and an impressive mural in Norbulingka provides a brief illustration of the entire Tibetan history, from the origination of Tibetans to the 14th Dalai Lama's meeting with Chairman Mao.

Social Murals

Some murals are neither religious nor historical, but rather feature the social life of Tibetans. For example, in Jokhang Temple , there is a group of jubilation murals that shows people singing, dancing, playing musical instruments and engaging in sporting matches. In Potala and Samye Monastery , murals of folk sport activities and acrobatics can also be seen.

In addition, many large palaces or temples in Tibet feature murals that describe their entire architectural design and construction process. These murals can be found in Potala, Jokhang, Samye Temple, Sakya Monastery and other famous buildings in Tibet.

Whether religious, historical or social, all of the murals are elaborate and detailed pieces created by expert artists. In some cases, strict guidelines define the correct way that a key figure should be depicted, so the artist must use his artistic talents to impart subtle differences that will make the mural unique from others that feature the same figure. Colors must be applied properly to make sure the murals do not fade excessively over time

Bullboat Dancing

Bullboat dancing is a kind of folk art that has passed down generation by generation in Junpa, a small Tibetan hamlet. Nowadays, the dancing regained its vitality with the fast development of the tourism industry.

Junpa is a small village located in Quxu County, 50 kilometers away from Lhasa, capital of Tibet Autonomous Region. With its time-honored history, the village is known for being the only fishing village left in Tibet, even on the whole Tibet Plateau. Therefore, it has become a hot tourism destination alluring tourists from home and aboard. Bullboat dancing is one of its performances to introduce Tibetan culture and woo travelers.

Rutog rock paintings in western Tibet

The famous bird-observing site, Pangongcuo Lake, is surrounded by rocks on which there are many paintings. They are the well-known Rutog rock paintings in western Tibet. Some of them are on the rocks beside the road. You can easily see them in your car if you travel to Ngari, west Tibet. But these are newly painted in the past years. You should get off the road to view those valuable and ancient rock paintings at Rutog

Recently, people find a large number of rock paintings in the Gerze, Ge'gyai and Rutog counties. Some of them are found in higher elevations in western and northern Tibet. Deep and shallow lines are carved on stones with hard rocks or other hard objects. Some pictures were even painted in rich colors. The most beautiful rock paintings are discovered at a dozen places in the Rutog County. Among them, those in the Risum Rimodong and Lorinaka are both large in size and great in number. Their artistic value is also tremendous.

Rock art belongs to the stone carving culture. In ancient times, Tibetan people used the stone inscriptions to describe and record their way of life and work during the early development of human society. The content of the Rutog rock paintings are very rich, including hunting, religious ritual, riding, domestic animal herding and farming, and objects like the sun and moon, mountains, yaks, horses, sheep, donkeys, antelopes, houses, figures, etc. This is simple and natural. For us, those inscriptions are precious cultural record from human ancestors.

The capital of the ancient Xiangxiong Kingdom was also in the Ngari. Xiangxiong writing is a special form of writing created by the ancestors of the Tibetan ethnic group. This kind of writing is significant as it appeared before Tibetan writing. Thus, the rock paintings here are very important to study the history, culture and early human life in Ngari, as well as the whole region of Tibet. Therefore, tourists are kindly required to protect these rock paintings at Rutog, these precious presents from human ancestor

Tibetan Cuisine

When traveling to Tibet, of course, you can't miss the Tibetan food and sweet tea. Tibetan food is an important part of Chinese cuisine.

Tibetan food is characterized by varied cooking of yak meat, mutton, milk product, highland barley and potato. To stew, braise, simmer, steam, fry and roast are the main ways of cooking dishes, while the staple food are made by steaming, boiling or frying.

There are many types of dishes in Tibet. While the best place to enjoy them, I believe, is Lhasa, for Lhasa is the capital city as well as the biggest city of Tibet. Some of the dishes can be very expensive, while most of them are not. You can certainly find delicious dishes at reasonable cost. The most popular dishes are Tibetan momo, stewed chicken with Chinese caterpillar fungus, a traditional herb which can also be stewed with beef. Then, there are fried mutton ribs, roast lamb leg, air-dried meat, cold yak tongue, fried beef ribs, Tibetan sausage, potato curry, stewed beef and turnip, braised beef, steamed dumplings stuffed with beef, zamba, steamed bread stuffed with potato, rice curry, ginseng sweet rice and various kinds of desserts.

As a typical Tibetan food, the zamba is made by grinding the fried highland barley flour, which boasts a good smell and taste. It's easy to carry and there are many ways to eat it. Thus it is widely considered the best food for a traveler. The Tibetans use silver or high-quality porcelain dinner wares to serve dishes, while the most common ones are wooden.

Monks are some of the most revered members of society here in Tibet. And since we are what we eat, we're digging into the details of a traditional Tibetan monks' diet in an effort to become more like these men we hold in such high esteem

The Most Beloved Food and Beverage in Tibet

Travellers look for different things, when they visit a place. Food is one of the most important things among that and the cuisine makes a place even more appealing. Tibetan cuisine is unique and the geography of the place and the neighbouring countries influence it greatly. From noodles and cheese to butter and soups, Tibetan food is absolutely wonderful. Travellers will love the taste of the various dishes and there are some amazing restaurants, which offer good service and mouth-watering preparations. Various grains are used as Tibet's staple food and barley is quite common. Dairy products along with milk are almost indispensable and people consume them quite often. Tibet doesn't produce rice in huge amounts, so it comes from the imports. The southern region witnesses some rice cultivation, but it is not sufficient to feed the entire region.

How does the unique topography of Tibet influence its agriculture and lifestyle?

Agriculture heavily depends on the climate and this is same for Tibet as well. The extreme high altitude makes it difficult to cultivate vegetables and fresh fruits, so we have resorted to other products. We locals formed our cuisine, based on the available things and this shaped our lifestyle. When the winter becomes extreme, survival is extremely tough and agriculture almost comes to a standstill. Tibetan cuisine is different from other regions, though it is delicious and nutritious. Modern agricultural procedures are now slowly being introduced and this has changed the condition massively. Greenhouses were constructed and many crops were grown inside them. Tibetan vegetative conditions show a great deal of variation, so the cuisine is not the same throughout.

In the high hilly areas, Tibetan crops can't be grown and they are cultivated in the low regions. Barley's importance is huge in Tibet. It is not only easy to grow, it is widely acceptable too. Tsampa and Sha Phaley are eaten by most people and Balep is perfect for breakfast as well as lunch. Dinners can be delicious too, as Tibetans prefer Thukpa at that time. This item is extremely delicious and it is extremely healthy too. Thukpa is prepared by mixing meat, vegetables and different varieties of noodles and forming a soup. There is a lot to learn from the Tibetan lifestyle and our attention to detail is amazing. We take each job seriously and show our unique culture in the littlest of things.Bamboo chopsticks are used to serve the cuisine in Tibet. This is different from that of Himalayan cuisine, as that is eaten by hand.

Best Tibetan Foods:

1. Tsampa

Tsampa is Tibet's staple item and this nutty-tasting foodstuff is prepared from delicious roasted barley. This item is extremely unique and exclusive to Tibet. The grain has deep roots in Tibetan culture and the locals are often refereed as tsampa-eaters. A food item can be used to represent the people of a place and that is exactly what has happened here

Main Ingredients: Roasted flour is the main ingredient and wheat flour is also used at times. The entire mixture is often blended with Tibet's butter tea, which is a bit salty in nature.

Making of Tsampa: Tibetans prefer food, which are very convenient to make. The preparation process is quite simple and nomads as well as travelers eat it a lot. Traditionally tea is one of the main ingredients, but now beer and water is also used. Initially, a bowl needs to be taken and buttered tea is kept at the very bottom. A sufficient amount of tsampa is dropped on it and then the mixture is stirred well. A dumpling-like paste is formed and that it is washed down with more tea. The preparation poses many challenges and dexterity needs to be shown. Moreover, to make it delicious, practical experience is a must. Perfection comes slowly, as the things need to be mixed in right proportions.

Cultural significance of Tsampa: Apart from being a major role in Tibet's diet, the religious significance of tsampa is also noteworthy. Some Buddhist rituals involve throwing of tsampa, as an offering to gods. The food item got intermingled with Tibet's culture and it denotes joy and ecstatic celebrations. Tsampa is widely used during the New Year and it brings good luck to everyone. In Buddhist funerals, tsampa-throwing occurs and it helps in releasing the dead person's soul.

2. Chang

In the snowy lands of Tibet, barley wine or Chang can keep you warm. This alcoholic beverage is famous here and it's widely consumed in the neighboring communities as well

Main Ingredients: This relative of the world famous beer are brewed with the help of barley, millet and rice grains.

Making of Chang: The millet seeds are stuffed inside a barrel in semi-fermented condition and then hot water is poured on to it. A narrow bamboo tube known as pipsing is used to let the water pass. As this boiled barley cools down, yeast is added and the mixture is kept for 2-3 days to intensify the fermentation. The fermentation ends after the given time frame and water is again added to make it ready for drinking.

Usage of Chang: In Tibet's social structure, Chang is often given to guests to welcome them. They are used in religious occasions too. Chang has a great cultural significance and it is often used a tool to settle disputes. In the liquor market of the world, Tibet has made its contribution by introducing 'Lhasa Beer'. Lhasa Brewing Company convinced international investors and increased networks to make this product famous.

3. Yak Butter

Yak is domesticated in many areas of Tibet and yak butter is obtained from the female species. This staple product is imported outside and herding communities use it frequently. Not only butter, but a lot of other dairy products are prepared from Yak's milk.

Main Ingredients: Prepared from Yak's milk, this butter is also used in a special variety of Tibetan tea. In the scenic mountain pastures yak's milk is converted into butter and it has a great market value.

Making of Yak Butter: Individual yaks don't produce a sufficient amount of milk and this is why large herds are useful. Milk is obtained in huge amounts in summer, as compared to winter. The milk is left for fermentation for a night and then the resulting substance is churned. In winter, the accumulated yoghurt is laid on a sheep's stomach and a butter form is formed.

Cultural Significance of Yak Butter: Yak butter supplements tsampa and they are eaten together. Apart from dominating the diet in a major way, Yak's butter has become an indispensable part of Tibet's culture and religious practices. The prayer wheels are lubricated by using it and the lamps use it as a fuel. Moreover, in the butter lamp festival, the lamps make use of this product to remain illuminated. Sculptures made of butter flower are absolutely stunning and they are sold in many exhibitions in Tibet.

4. Tibetan Yoghurt

Any kind of yoghurt is delicious, but Tibetan yoghurt is extremely delicious. Tourists can taste this delicious item, when they come here and treat their delicate taste buds

Main Ingredients: Instead of cow milk, yak's milk is used to prepare this yoghurt. The butterfat content is higher in this milk, so this yoghurt becomes extremely creamy.

Making of Tibetan Yoghurt: Yak's precious milk is taken and it is boiled in the initial stage. Then it is left for cooling and the fermentation process begins. The flavor is extremely strong and people love it for the taste. Tibetan yoghurt is available in every cities and this desert is extremely famous.

Cultural Significance of Tibetan Yoghurt: Tibetan's eat yoghurt in the Shoton festival and it is an old tradition. Yoghurt festival is celebrated widely and tourists can taste the amazing delicacy by visiting Tibet.

Tibetans are greatly enthusiastic about the food and they love experimenting new things. Explore the amazing picturesque region of Tibet and get mesmerized by the amazing dishes.

Tibetan Momo, A Kind of Exotic Dumpling in Tibet

One Chinese proverb says: "Food is the first necessity of the people." That's exactly true. Food always best represents the real life and culturein a place and it also directly reflects the flavor preference of the natives, as the Sichuan people prefer spicy dishes, Hong Kong Citizens, sweet soups, etc. There is a kind of exotic dumpling in Tibet named Momo that meets with great favor in neighboring Nepal, the Kingdom of Bhutan and even New York City. Why does this ordinary Tibetan wheaten food become so popular overseas? What's the special unknown reason behind it? Is it any particular about the cooking, way to eat, ingredients or side dishes? Hereby, let's reveal the mysterious veil on this Tibetan cuisine.

What is Momo?

As a traditional wheaten food in Tibet, Momo may look like Chinese dumpling or Baozi. However, don't be cheated by its dumpling-like shape because it is different from dumpling. Momo derives from Tibet but it is even more popular in Nepal, which always misleads people to consider Momo originates from Nepal. Actually the majority of Tibetan momo is half-moon in shape, however Nepali one is normally round and filled with chicken, coriander, ginger, and Nepali spice. Momo can be cooked in various ways including steam, fry, and boil; therefore the different cooking methods will bring you different sense of taste.

Just like that common Chinese dumplings dip in vinegar, momo usually dips in its special sauce, made of tomato sauce and mustard. Fried momo dipped with this sauce fantastically tastes like the flavor of curry. What an amazing magic! Since momo flavor is acceptable and loved by almost everyone from all the nations and regions and, its making and cooking method is not too difficult for ordinary people to try it in their kitchen. Then nowadays, it becomes so popular all around world that some American families even "invent" their own Tibetan momos at home. For this reason, let's have our momo DIY either and try to cook the Tibetan momo of our own.

DIY our momo

Tibetan momo can be filled with pork, chicken, beef or mutton. Every Tibetan family has a slightly different momo recipe, with various theories on how to make them. Then we can give full play of our intelligence and create the unique Tibetan momo of our own.

1. Make the dough

Dough is the basic to momo as ABC to English. The dough quality will directly impact the momo flavor. So mix the flour and water very well by hand and keep adding water until you make a pretty smooth ball of dough. This is the first and very important step. Use about 2 cups of wheat flour and blend it with between 3/4 cups and 1 cup of water. Considering different types of flours, you don't need to measure this ratio too accurately. Then knead the dough very well until the dough is flexible. Now leave your dough in the pot with a lid or one piece of wet cloth on it while you prepare the rest of the ingredients because you should not let the dough dry out, or it will be hard to work with

2. The filling

Momo can be filled with either meat or vegetable. In Tibet, people often use yak meat to fill momo, however for those who don't live in Tibet, they can also fill momo with beef, pork, mutton or chicken. For vegetable momo, chop all ingredients into very tiny pieces:

1.Two onions

2.Two or three cloves of garlic

3.A bunch of cilantro

4.One pound of cabbage

5.One quarter pound of dark brown mushrooms

6. Two tablespoons of soy sauce

7. One teaspoon of chicken, beef or vegetable bouillon

For vegetable fillings, add about 2 pounds of minced meat. If you have enough time, you can also chop the meat with gingers and garlics that will bring you a better sense of flavor. Moreover, add one or two rough eggs in the filling will dramatically enhance the mouth feel.

For both kinds of momos, put all the ingredients in a pot or big bowl, add a few salt or soybean sauce in accordance with personal taste and mix them thoroughly until every ingredient is mixing together very well. You can use a big spoon or fork or a pair of chopsticks for the blending, it is also acceptable to use your hand to mix it up if you are making meat filling.

3. Make the momo

As the dough and filling are both ready, it's the happy and magic time to make the momo. Place the dough on a chopping board and use a rolling pin to roll it out, be careful, don't roll it too thin if you are about to boil the momos. After the dough has been rolled out, you need to cut it into little round pieces for each momo. The easiest way to do this is turn a small cup or glass upside down to cut out circles about the size of the palm of your hand. If you feel too tough to roll the whole dough out, there is another option. Cut the dough into relatively small balls, and roll each ball in your palms until you have a smooth ball of dough, and then shape them into thin and slim cylinders by hands about 2 cm in diameter. Cut the flour cylinder into small ones with approximately 2 cm in height and roll each of them out for every momo.

Since all preparations are completed, now let's began to shape our momos. There are mainly two shapes of momo, round and half – moon. We are supposed to choose the second option as it stands for a more decent Tibetan style. Now hold the flat circular dough in one hand (left hand for major people) and put a tablespoon of filling in the middle of the dough. Then fold the circle of dough in half, covering over the filling and press together the two edges of the half circle so that there is no open edge in the half circle, ensuring the filling is completely enclosed in the dough. You can also make your momo prettier by pinching and folding along the curved edge of the half circle. Now a cute half – moon momo is born in your hands. How wonderful! Repeat this method for more momos and place them on a non-stick surface and put a damp cloth or lid handy on them to keep the momos you've made from drying out while you're finishing the others.

4. Cook the momo

As momo can be cooked in various ways, here we only introduce one popular and easy cooking method for both Chinese and foreigners: Fry momo.

Heat rape oil in a medium-sized pan over medium heat. Once the oil heats up, you should place some momos in the pan, trying to move them apart enough so that to prevent them from sticking together. Fry the momos for 2-3 minutes until the dough turn into light brown. Add 50 milliliters of water to the pan and heat it over high heat. Cover the pan and until the water was completely evaporated. Then, open the pan and turn the heat back to medium. Add some oil to the pan and fry them until they are crispy with golden brown bottoms. Once the momos were cooked, it is suggested to place them on a plate with a paper towel on it to absorb the excess oil.

5. Make Momo Dipping Sauce

Considering that momo can be paired with numerous sipping sauces and it will taste peculiar while sipping in different sauces, such as chili paste, curry sauce, lemon spices, etc. Hereby we only introduce the most popular sipping sauce in China, with two grades, the "simple "one and the "luxury" one. Combine soy sauce and vinegar blending with tomato sauce and curry. Then it completes the "simple" dipping sauce. For a "luxury" one, you can also add a few sugar, peppers, ajinomoto, sesame oil, shallots and garlic.

6. Eat the momo

Now pick one cute momo and sip it in the sauce and put it in your mouth. What an astonishing experience, isn't it?

So, make your move and start to DIY the momo special to your own. This unique flavor will fly you to Tibet in no time even though you are sitting beside your dinner table at home. Furthermore, don't forget to taste the authentic Tibetan momo when you are touring in Tibet.

The Most Significant Tibetan Culture: Sweet Tea House in Lhasa

Sweet tea to Tibetans is just like coffee to Westerners. Most Tibetans get used to making a sip of sweet tea in the morning and their dinners are paired by sweet tea either, and some of them even don't drink water but only sweet tea. In Lhasa, the sweet tea house is not merely ordinary tea house, in a large sense it's a place for information collection, socializing, moreover it also serves as the local news forum.

History of Tibetan Sweet Tea

Sweet tea doesn't originate from Tibet. About one century ago, some Islamic business persons who shuttled from Nepal and India to Tibet brought the sweet tea in and some riches and politically influential families in Tibet for the first time tasted it. Ever since then, Tibetan aristocrats have been found of sweet tea and some of them even hired special cooks from Nepal or India to make sweet tea for them, therefore, this kind of beverage was soon popular among the Tibetan aristocrats and the act that treat the guests with sweet tea became a representation of the hosts' hospitality. Until 1920s, only nobilities, riches, and aristocrats were allowed into sweet houses in Lhasa.

In Tibet, females are usually more skillful of making sweet tea and even every woman in Lhasa knows the sweet tea making method, ironically, before 1980s, women were not allowed into sweet tea houses, which was a total forbidden place for them, at that time if a woman ever entered a sweet tea house, rumors will immediately spread all over the city and her family members will be suffered and ashamed of this movement either.

Another decades passed, sweet tea houses can be found everywhere in Lhasa, their business was booming. As women have been acquiesced to enter sweet tea houses by far, almost every citizen in Lhasa likes to take a rest in sweet tea houses in afternoon. Now it has become a stylish popular scene in sweet tea houses that groups of young men, Tibetan Buddhists, senior citizens, women gather at each table, speaking the stories of their own. Nowadays, as Tibet continually opens up to the outside world and economy keeps souring, sweet tea, the once aristocracy privilege beverage, has become the drink for everyone. Today, for Lhasa citizens, sweet house is still the place for information exchange and it also provides Lhasa citizens a public cozy place of socializing. In sweet tea house, Tibetans casually spend their leisure time in the fragrant, aroma and sweet scent pervading from the pots of boiling fluid on ovens that has become an inseparable part of Tibetan lives.

Tibetans in Sweet Tea House

As the most popular Tibetan beverage and one of staple foods, sweet tea means "Qabadi" in Tibetan is made of black tea, mixing with milk and sugar, serving as refreshment. The fact that Tibetans are keen on sweet tea generates numbers of sweet tea houses in Lhasa, the capital of Tibet Autonomous Region. People in Lhasa always kill their leisure time in sweet houses. Though a panorama view in sweet tea houses, we can see: senior citizens are discussing family issues, echoed by laughters; groups of young men are playing Xiu, a traditional Tibetan dicing game, in which players can "kill" each other, lingering around excitement.

Sweet tea house also provides a rest area for Tibetan Buddhists. Lamas spin their prayer wheels in one hand while hold the tea cup in another murmuring the Buddhist texts and meditating ever now and then. In sweet tea house, costumers always put several small amount amounts of cash (usually 0.5 or 0.6 RMB) on the table and waiters will fill their cup accordingly. Everybody loves this public space, they discuss social news, beliefs, lives and business, the atmosphere there is lively, joyful, friendly and cozy. In Lhasa, the sweet tea house is not in a society, it is the tiny Tibetan society, and furthermore, it also symbolizes the slow and relaxed life style in Lhasa. People in the sweet tea house are all basking in their exclusive happiness. For this reason, tourists to Lhasa should never miss the sweet tea house.

Most Popular Sweet Tea Houses in Lhasa:

Most tourists cannot get used to the Tibetan buttered tea, but few to the sweet tea. We hereby recommend some popular and stylish sweet tea houses in Lhasa, and sincerely hope you can have a good and exotic charming time there.

1. CangGusi Sweet Tea House

As an authentic Tibet tea house, through the narrow gate, the suddenly enlightened backyard will immediately attract your interest. Though, CangGusi sweet tea house is small in size, it's always filled with local senior citizens, and the sweet scent diffuses from the tea pots on the kitchen oven, people's voices mingled with spinning prayer wheels sound create this tea house an astonishing static merry go around. Take your time, select a comfortable seat and taste a cup of sweet tea here, these agreeable moments will never be erased from your memory.

Tips:

No smoking in the tea house.

Specialties here include yak meat, Tibetan noodles, sweet tea, buttered tea, bean jelly, beef noodles.

2. Guang Ming Sweet Tea House

This traditional Tibetan tea house is hiding in the depth of an ally, composed of three parts, one outdoor and two indoor. There's nothing luxury, but natural and wild, old style tables and chairs silently recount all time washed stories, it's just like a time tunnel, through which you can suddenly escape from the fast paced life and immerse in the slow life featured with Tibetan style. Most costumers here are local males and they are all familiar with each other. For them, this sweet tea house serves as their information and news center that is just like in old days when government used to post their decrees in the tea houses so as to most effectively publicize the policy. Nowadays, if you understand Tibetan language, Guang Ming Sweet Tea Houses would also be the best access to the latest Tibetan news.

Since there's no usher, costumers should take tea cups by themselves, and put 0.6 or 0.7 RMB on the table, waiters then will fill your cup accordingly, no conversation is in need, it's a kind of tacit understanding. Find a seat by the window and sit at leisure, watch pedestrians passing by outside, harvest a satisfaction in heart.

3. Luo Qu Sweet Tea House

Specializing in sweet tea and Tibetan noodles, Luo Qu Sweet Tea House is a popular place for local citizens. Before you are considering where to take the tea cup, the house owner has been greeting you with enthusiasm already. One smallest pot of sweet tea will only cost you 5 RMB and here is also the place suffused with authentic Tibetan atmosphere.

4. Shan Dong Sweet Tea House

As it is located in a cave near the famous Potala Palace, many lamas and tourists will visit here after the shrine worship or palace tour. Besides its great geographic location, Shan Dong sweet tea house is also featured with special scenery, the cave, through which streams of gloomy, dim light penetrate from outside and caste on all kinds of faces, in the air, Tibetan conversations echo with boiled tea fluid purrs, composing a wonderful cozy leisure ambient.

5. Ni Ma Tea House

Featuring as one of local citizen's favorite tea houses, few tourists will appear in Ni Ma Tea House, therefore, here is one of the best places to experience the decent Tibetan lives and sweet tea culture. Despite the humble decoration, the authentic sweet tea flavor and Tibetan dessert will capture your mind through your stomach and let you forget you are traveling here. Ni Ma Tea House also provides decent Tibetan noodles; hence you win a chance to taste the ingenuous Tibetan food here.

Last But not the Least

One old proverb indicates: "When in Rome, do as Romans do." Sweet tea, the most popular and essential drinks for Tibetans, all tourists in Lhasa should also "drink as Tibetans do." So take one afternoon of doing nothing, but sitting beside one old table in a sweet tea house, then slowly drink your tea out, intoxicating yourself in the typical sweet Tibetan charming

Steven Willis

Tibetan People

There are three major groups of people in Qinghai-Tibet Plateau, namely, Tibetan nomads, peasants and urban residents.

The living style of Tibetan nomads hasn't changed a lot since the kingdom of Songtsen Gampo in the 7th century. They always wear Tibetan leather robes and lead a nomadic life in the northern Tibet. Many herdsmen have never been to the towns until their death. Their tanned skin, strong physique and noble manner remind tourists of American Indians. Women in grazing area usually comb their hair into many small plaits, then bundle them into a larger braid hanging after necks and decorate with colored stones. Some of them also cover their hair with a big patch of cloth sewn on copper-coins and shells. Every step they take, all the decorations clink together. As winter sets in Tibet, they head down to the valley of Yarlung Zangbo River and exchange for daily necessities like tea, barley, etc. With the first ray of spring, all the families move back to the north again.

Compared with Tibetans living in the south, shepherds have a wider choice in food. Domestic sheep, yak and antelope on the prairie provide them with plenty protein and fat. The fat is called as ghee, which plays a key role in making Tibetan butter tea. In addition to various sorts of meat, they also enjoy goat's milk and Tibetan yogurt freely. Having hundreds of sheep and yak, Tibetan nomads can live a self-sufficient life. How lucky they are!

Tibetan farmers often wear dark brown or grey robe made of Pulu (a woolen fabric). Relatively speaking, Tibetan peasants make a more stable life but have lots to concern. They can only produce barley, turnip and potatoes on this pool soil. Raising cattle has been their subsidiary business. However, cattles couldn't grow very well under such a harsh environment and what they can eat is straw. Thus, the limited milk, ghee and cheese become precious in Tibet farming area.

For most females, the ability to make Tibetan tea is an especially needed skill. And among all kinds of tea, Sichuan tea is Tibetan's favorite. They brew tea with soda in a small amount of water, then put together with ghee, salt and boiled water into a wooden barrel, and stir them vigorously with a long stick for about five minutes. Tea is not only regarded as Tibetan beverage, but also a staple food for Tibetans. As for many poor people, they think it's too luxurious for them to put ghee while making tea. Therefore, they only add a small slice of ghee in their cups and drink cautiously to blow the oil on the surface aside, finally mix with zanba.

Urban residents like businessmen, government officials and handicraftsmen pay more attention to their dressing. Males usually wear cotton or silk shirt in their robes. Poor or rich, they'll put a piece of turquoise on the right ear to show their elegance. Upon the arrival of Tibetan festivals, females in the urban area would dress in brocade clothes and rainbow aprons. Their leisure life can be described as follows: getting up at six to eight o'clock and then worshipping Gods. After washing hands, the host or hostess spring holy water around repeat "an-ma-yan" three times to purify environment. Finally, they sit down to chant Buddhist scripture.

All the Tibetan people can't live without three mascots, that is, Buddha, Buddhist teachings, and Tibetan monks (lamas), which are believed to bring them blessing and harmony. They also hold that Mount Kailash is the center of the world and all the lives are circling around the carriers of holiness. And those sacred carries can be mountains, lakes, stupas, temples, etc. That's the reason why you can see many pilgrims prostrating in front of Jokhang Monastery and circumambulating it day and night.

As the old saying goes, seeing is believing. Join our Tibet tour to know more about Tibet and people living here and uncover the great Himalayan mystery: the Yeti !

Lhoba People in Sountheast of Himalayas

If you want to experience a small window to distant hunter-gatherer past of our species, Tibet offers a surprising and unique experience: The Lhoba people. Lhoba people are the smallest of the 56 ethnic groups in China and live in South-eastern Tibet. Most of these sourherners (Lhoba means "southerners" in Tibetan language) do not traditionally self-identify as a single entity and speak different languages but considered the same Lhoba minority by Chinese and Tibetans. Lhoba population consists of many tribes; Bogar, Ningbo, Adi and Tajin peoples to name some. Today there are about 4000 Lhoba people in China but many Lhoba people also live in northeast India, Bhutan and Myanmar

History of Lhoba and their living environment

Unfortunately, not much is known about the history and origin of Lhoba people. Because the Lhoba language do not have a written script and prior to 1950s all Lhoba people were illiterate, almost nothing is written by Lhoba people about their culture and history. Living in one of the most mountainous region and being one of the most isolated human group in the world also do not help.

We know that the Southern regions of Tibet were once occupied by India but in 7th century, Tibet succeeded unifying tribes and started to real this region as well as the rest of the Tibet. But, it is not known the ancestors of Lhoba people were occupying the region at that time or came from somewhere else later.

What we know for sure is that from the conquest of Tibet to 1950s, Lhoba people were frequently bullied and oppressed by the Tibetans. Under the strict feudal society of Tibet, Lhoba people were considered inferior and "wild". They were not allowed to leave their area without permission and were not allowed to marry Tibetans.

Language and religion of Lhoba

Although there are only 5 to 6 thousand Lhoba people in the world, they have surprisingly large language diversity. Lhoba speaks Sino-Tibetan languages named Adi and Bokar; as well as Idu Mishmi. These languages are not mutually intelligible and Lhoba people do not have any written script.

Most Lhoba people are animist but a significant portion of the population believes in Tibetan Buddhism (although they still mix animist traditions with this relatively new religion). As animists, Lhoba people believe that everything has an immortal spirit called "Wuyong". The concept of Wuyong has a significant influence on the life and work of Lhoba people. All living things in the world are subject to wuyong and it brings bad fortune to offend a wuyong. The Lhoba people are very superstitious and have many taboos related to Wuyong.

Lhoba religion also has various natural gods. Their main god is tiger which is the most dangerous animal in the region. There are 30 totems and gods in the religion like the mountain, the tree, dog, pig, leopard, bear, pig, moon, sun and ox.

Lhoba religion practices include shamanism, spiritual healing, fortune-telling and wizardry. The Lhoba fortune-telling practice is quite unique as they read patterns (colour, shape and blood vessels) in a freshly harvested liver. Oddly shaped blood vessels on this freshly harvested liver are bad omens.

Customs and dress, cuisine and life style of Lhoba

The customs and dress of Lhoba people vary by tribes and region. But in general, Lhoba men clothing reflects their hunting lifestyle. They wear knee-length, sleeveless, buttonlessblack jackets made of sheep's wool with hats made from bear skin or bamboo stripes. The men also wear swords and carry bows and arrows. Lhoba women wears skirts made from sheep's wool and narrow-sleeved blouses. Both men and women do not wear shoe ware

Although the diet varies in different regions, roasting is the most popular way of cooking. They roast both animal and plant based food. The popular way of cooking is putting the game in fire and covering by ashes to prepare for eating. Other than the game they hunt, they consume maize or millet flourdumplings, rice or buckwheat. The communities near Tibetan people, the cuisine also includes potatoes and spicy food.

In old days, Lhoba people were divided into two classes - "maide" and "nieba". The maides considered themselves nobles and saw the niebas inferior and at their disposal. The maides were allowed to hold nieba slaves and even if a nieba became rich, he could not be considered maide

Today, most Lhoba live at the foot of the Himalayas, in the high mountains and deep valleys. Thickly forested area is sparsely populated. The region is called Pemako. Lhoba lives in villages on high terraces. Since the area does not allow grain cultivation, until very recently, most Lhoba people depended on hunting. Very basic agriculture to supplement hunting was practiced. Today, most Lhoba people are Lhoba households are farmers but hunting is the central activity of Lhoba men. Starting from a very young age, and young boys start to join adults in hunting. As they mature, they hunt animals in deep forest alone or by teams. Even today, hunting dogs play a significant part in Lhoba life and it is common for a family to own dozens of dogs which are taken into homes as family.

The barter animal hides, musk, bear paws and other items with Tibetans in exchange for tools and clothing. The life for Lhoba people are harsh due to the region they live and most Lhoba people are considered poor in the region. The Pemako area can be reached after weeks of jeep and foot travel so the people are still pretty much isolated.

One interesting fact about Lhoba people is that they do not lock their doors. Stealing and lying are considered heavy crimes and stealing is punished heavily, usually expelling from the village. Reoffenders are executed.

Lhoba societies are patriarchal and in the feudal past, women had no rights and had inherited nothing from their husbands and fathers. The society practices monogamy and polygamy.

On what occasion (festival or places) can tourists experience Lhoba culture and customs

Lately, tourism became a significant source of income for Lhoba people. Today, one of the most important Lhoba settlement is Caizhao Village, which is created by resettling mountain villages in 1985. Caizhao Village now has a small village with Lhoba features, a folk customs museum. Village square is also an important place to experience Lhoba culture and customs as Lhoba regularly gather in the village square to perform their Dances and Songs for (small) Tourist Groups.

Annual Lhoba Ethnic Custom Festival of Nanyigou Township is the best way to experience Lhoba culture. Attracting large number of tourists, many dance and song teams in traditional costumes perform during the festival.

Xudulong Festival is the most special Lhoba festival which is celebrated on the second month of Tibetan calendar. Known as Donggeng Gurumu (meaning something like "congratulate the safety of the current year and look forward to a bumper harvest in the coming year"), the festival witnesses Lhoba people butchering cattle and pigs to be given as presents to the maternal relatives. The skull of the consumed animal is held in front of the houses to symbolize diligence and wealth

Today, most Lhoba people celebrate The New Year Festival but their celebration date and style is different than typical Tibetan. The new year is celebrated three times, as each harvest is seen as a different year (on November the 1st, December the 1st and January). All Lhoba tribes celebrate The New Year after heavy harvesting and many also like to hold wedding ceremonies during the new year celebrations.

Where you can Meet Lhoba People when Taking a Tibet Tour

Presnetly, most of Lhoba people are living in Nanyi Valley of Milin County, Nyingchi, Damu town of Motuo County, Yu town of Longzi County, Shannan and other two around places. For the tourists, we couldn't meet them for a regular Tibet tour because of isolation and quarantine.

Uncovering the great Himalayan mystery: the Yeti

When we think about the Himalayan mountains, we can't help but conjure up in our minds the image of a tall, ape-like man with shaggy, white fur, quite likely running around with a bat in his hands. That's right, we're talking about none other than the Yeti. You know, that figure we all came to know, love and simultaneously fear as children. We have popular programs like *Doctor Who* and *Scooby Doo* to thank for that, not to mention the countless films of the late 20th century on "Big Foot," which is essentially the American, Hollywood version of this ancient, Himalayan figure.

So, how did the Yeti come into being? Is there any validity to the claims that it actually exists? We're about to dig into all of that.

The Origin Story

Like most ancient facets of Tibetan culture, the Yeti's genesis is rooted in religion, specifically the pre-Buddhist religion Bön. Those that adhered to this faith prayed to a hunting god, who they deemed the ruler of the forests' creatures. This god would come to be known as the Yeti, but during this time, it was the "Glacier Being."

Like in any religion, spiritual ceremonies were organized in order to honour this deity of theirs. Rituals included, first and foremost, making an annual sacrifice to him—done so that the people would be sure to receive the protection of this Glacier Being. A proper ceremony involved the sacrificed animal being placed on the ground, in a particular position that allowed for its intestines to be facing up. The hunter would then crouch behind the animal and pray aloud in a soft, slow manner while gathering the intestines and throwing them over the animal's head

Other religious rituals involved the mixing of the Glacier Being's precious blood with mustard and poison to create a magical concoction. This was only possible, of course, once they had hunted the creature. The fact that they could acquire his blood meant that, though he was viewed as divine, he was also a very real, physical entity.

This at once spiritual and corporeal creature is believed by the people of Nepal to have the ability to live a very long time—some have even claimed to have seen him in recent years. Before opening that can of worms though, let's take a look at how the mythological Yeti emerged out of this spiritual Glacier Being.

The Yeti in Mythology

Some say that the term "Yeti" stems from the Sherpa word "yeh-teh," a descriptive term meaning "small, man-like animal" that may have been used to refer to the creature. Still, others claim that the name is derived from the Sherpa word "meti," which means bear.

In any case, the figure developed out of the original, godly role it once played, into this mythic one of today when it began to be utilized in Tibetan folklore. From the start, these legends depicted the Yeti as a dangerous figure, one to be avoided unless you wanted to welcome in misfortune to your life.

Traditionally, the tales would be recounted by the community's elders, around whom everyone would gather and hear all about this wild snowman. Children, in particular, were meant to be the target audience, as their parents wished to dissuade them from wandering off on their own. While, everyone was meant to take away from the stories the warning that approaching wild animals is a risky act.

The terrible nature of the Yeti was always emphasized in his physical description: large, shaggy-haired, with immensely-sized feet that left enormous footprints in the snow. Plus he was said to never be without his menacing, stony weapon.

Popular Tales about Himalayan Yeti
Annihilation of the Yeti
This is the story of a community of Sherpas who decide they will attempt to get revenge on a group of Yetis who had been mercilessly tormenting them for some time. Their plan of action involved drinking a lot of alcohol and then proceeding to engage in a "fight" amongst themselves—the trick was that this was an orchestrated brawl, not a real one. Their hope was that the Yetis would follow suit, and wind up actually destroying one another. This plan didn't succeed though in

the end. The wise Yetis were not fooled, and instead of defeating each other, they continued their expedition higher up in the mountains, wreaking havoc on even more Sherpa communities.

The Growing Yeti
In this legend, a man comes across a Yeti who is growing directly in front of his eyes. Taller and taller he becomes. The snowman's height increases at the speed of the sun's rising. As the man bears witness to this unusual site, he finds himself losing energy. In the end, he winds up falling unconscious.

Fact or Fiction?
There are tons of stories like those mentioned above floating around, and they beg the question, are these really just stories? Is it possible that the Yeti is real? The remaining Bön sect followers certainly believe so, and—it turns out—many others do, too. In fact, there have been a considerable amount of sightings claimed, even in recent years, hence all the Hollywood films we have today on the topic.

Notable Sightings of Yeti Incident
A number of individuals travel to the Himalayas just to try and see the Yeti in its natural habitat: in isolation, in the mountains. Here are some of the most significant sightings in recent history.

The 1921 British Expedition

Wonder where the term "abominable snowman" fits into the story of the Yeti/Glacier Being/Big Foot? Well, when the Brits explored Mount Everest in the early 20s, they came upon very large footprints in the snow. A sherpa told them these were the imprints of a "metoh-kangmi," which translates roughly to "man-bear snow-man." Later, when this expedition was covered by journalist Henry Newman, he made the mistake of translating "metoh" into "filthy" rather than "man-bear," and then decided instead of the word filthy, he would use "abominable." Thus was born the illusive Abominable Snowman, unseen but known for his very large footprints.

Reinhold Messner's 1980s Expedition
Called the most famous Yeti-hunter of all, Messner is known for having seen the Yeti during the 80s. He has since returned to the same spot in an effort to catch a glimpse of it again, but without any luck. However, it is his take on the mystery of the Yeti that really sets him apart from other Yeti-seekers. He claims it is not a crazy, half-human-half-bear, but in actuality, it's just a type of bear whose species has yet to be identified—a cross between a brown bear and a polar bear.

When it comes to sightings, there are a countless number of them every year, but none have yet to prove that the Yeti really exists. And according to the Nepalese, we shouldn't be looking. They warn that he's a whistling, growling beast that can kill you with a single punch, and if you come upon him, they say, you have no chance at survival. But if this doesn't deter you and you're really up for taking the gamble, bare in mind that the Yeti is allegedly a nocturnal creature. So if you want any chance at catching a glimpse of him, you'll have to try to do so during the nighttime. Stay safe, and happy hunting!

Steven Willis

Tibet and China history of a Complex Relationship
Is Tibet Part of China?

For at least 1500 years, the nation of Tibet has had a complex relationship with its large and powerful neighbor to the east, China. The political history of Tibet and China reveals that the relationship has not always been as one-sided as it now appears.

Indeed, as with China's relations with the Mongols and the Japanese, the balance of power between China and Tibet has shifted back and forth over the centuries.

Early Interactions

The first known interaction between the two states came in 640 A.D., when the Tibetan King Songtsan Gampo married the Princess Wencheng, a niece of the TangEmperor Taizong. He also married a Nepalese princess.

Both wives were Buddhists, and this may have been the origin of Tibetan Buddhism. The faith grew when an influx of Central Asian Buddhists flooded Tibet early in the eighth century, fleeing from advancing armies of Arab and Kazakh Muslims.

During his reign, Songtsan Gampo added parts of the Yarlung River Valley to the Kingdom of Tibet; his descendants would also conquer the vast region that is now the Chinese provinces of Qinghai, Gansu, and Xinjiang between 663 and 692. Control of these border regions would change hands back and forth for centuries to come.

In 692, the Chinese retook their western lands from the Tibetans after defeating them at Kashgar. The Tibetan king then allied himself with the enemies of China, the Arabs and eastern Turks.

Chinese power waxed strong in the early decades of the eighth century. Imperial forces under General Gao Xianzhi conquered much of Central Asia, until their defeat by the Arabs and Karluks at the Battle of Talas River in 751. China's power quickly waned, and Tibet resumed control of much of Central Asia.

The ascendant Tibetans pressed their advantage, conquering much of northern Indiaand even seizing the Tang Chinese capital city of Chang'an (now Xian) in 763.

Tibet and China signed a peace treaty in 821 or 822, which delineated the border between the two empires. The Tibetan Empire would concentrate on its Central Asian holdings for the next several decades, before splitting into several small, fractious kingdoms.

TIBET AND THE MONGOLS

Canny politicians, the Tibetans befriended Genghis Khan just as the Mongol leader was conquering the known world in the early 13th century. As a result, though the Tibetans paid tribute to the Mongols after the Hordes had conquered China, they were allowed much greater autonomy than the other Mongol-conquered lands.

Over time, Tibet came to be considered one of the thirteen provinces of the Mongolian-ruled nation of Yuan China.

During this period, the Tibetans gained a high degree of influence over the Mongols at court.

The great Tibetan spiritual leader, Sakya Pandita, became the Mongol's representative to Tibet. Sakya's nephew, Chana Dorje, married one of the Mongol Emperor Kublai Khan's daughters.

The Tibetans transmitted their Buddhist faith to the eastern Mongols; Kublai Khan himself studied Tibetan beliefs with the great teacher Drogon Chogyal Phagpa.

INDEPENDENT TIBET

When the Mongols' Yuan Empire fell in 1368 to the ethnic-Han Chinese Ming, Tibet reasserted its independence and refused to pay tribute to the new Emperor.

In 1474, the abbot of an important Tibetan Buddhist monastery, Gendun Drup, passed away. A child who born two years later was found to be a reincarnation of the abbot, and was raised to be the next leader of that sect, Gendun Gyatso.

After their lifetimes, the two men were called the First and Second Dalai Lamas. Their sect, the Gelug or "Yellow Hats," became the dominant form of Tibetan Buddhism.

The Third Dalai Lama, Sonam Gyatso (1543-1588), was the first to be so named during his life. He was responsible for converting the Mongols to Gelug Tibetan Buddhism, and it was the Mongol ruler Altan Khan who probably gave the title "Dalai Lama" to Sonam Gyatso.

While the newly-named Dalai Lama consolidated the power of his spiritual position, though, the Gtsang-pa Dynasty assumed the royal throne of Tibet in 1562. The Kings would rule the secular side of Tibetan life for the next 80 years.

The Fourth Dalai Lama, Yonten Gyatso (1589-1616), was a Mongolian prince and the grandson of Altan Khan.

During the 1630s, China was embroiled in power struggles between the Mongols, Han Chinese of the fading Ming Dynasty, and the Manchu people of north-eastern China (Manchuria). The Manchus would eventually defeat the Han in 1644, and establish China's final imperial dynasty, the Qing (1644-1912).

Tibet got drawn into this turmoil when the Mongol warlord Ligdan Khan, a Kagyu Tibetan Buddhist, decided to invade Tibet and destroy the Yellow Hats in 1634. Ligdan Khan died on the way, but his follower Tsogt Taij took up the cause.

The great general Gushi Khan, of the Oirad Mongols, fought against Tsogt Taij and defeated him in 1637. The Khan killed the Gtsang-pa Prince of Tsang, as well. With support from Gushi Khan, the Fifth Dalai Lama, Lobsang Gyatso, was able to seize both spiritual and temporal power over all of Tibet in 1642.

THE DALAI LAMA RISES TO POWER

The Potala Palace in Lhasa was constructed as a symbol of this new synthesis of power.

The Dalai Lama made a state visit to the Qing Dynasty's second Emperor, Shunzhi, in 1653. The two leaders greeted one another as equals; the Dalai Lama did not kowtow. Each man bestowed honors and titles upon the other, and the Dalai Lama was recognized as the spiritual authority of the Qing Empire.

According to Tibet, the "priest/patron" relationship established at this time between the Dalai Lama and Qing China continued throughout the Qing Era, but it had no bearing on Tibet's status as an independent nation. China, naturally, disagrees.

Lobsang Gyatso died in 1682, but his Prime Minister concealed the Dalai Lama's passing until 1696 so that the Potala Palace could be finished and the power of the Dalai Lama's office consolidated.

THE MAVERICK DALAI LAMA

In 1697, fifteen years after the death of Lobsang Gyatso, the Sixth Dalai Lama was finally enthroned.

Tsangyang Gyatso (1683-1706) was a maverick who rejected the monastic life, growing his hair long, drinking wine, and enjoying female company. He also wrote great poetry, some of which is still recited today in Tibet.

The Dalai Lama's unconventional lifestyle prompted Lobsang Khan of the Khoshud Mongols to depose him in 1705.

Lobsang Khan seized control of Tibet, named himself King, sent Tsangyang Gyatso to Beijing (he "mysteriously" died on the way), and installed a pretender Dalai Lama.

THE DZUNGAR MONGOL INVASION

King Lobsang would rule for 12 years, until the Dzungar Mongols invaded and took power. They killed the pretender to the Dalai Lama's throne, to the joy of the Tibetan people, but then began to loot monasteries around Lhasa.

This vandalism brought a quick response from the Qing Emperor Kangxi, who sent troops to Tibet. The Dzungars destroyed the Imperial Chinese battalion near Lhasa in 1718.

In 1720, the angry Kangxi sent another, larger force to Tibet, which crushed the Dzungars. The Qing army also brought the proper Seventh Dalai Lama, Kelzang Gyatso (1708-1757) to Lhasa.

THE BORDER BETWEEN CHINA AND TIBET

China took advantage of this period of instability in Tibet to seize the regions of Amdo and Kham, making them into the Chinese province of Qinghai in 1724.

Three years later, the Chinese and Tibetans signed a treaty that laid out the boundary line between the two nations. It would remain in force until 1910.

Qing China had its hands full trying to control Tibet. The Emperor sent a commissioner to Lhasa, but he was killed in 1750.

The Imperial Army then defeated the rebels, but the Emperor recognized that he would have to rule through the Dalai Lama rather than directly. Day-to-day decisions would be made on the local level.

ERA OF TURMOIL BEGINS

In 1788, the Regent of Nepal sent Gurkha forces to invade Tibet.

The Qing Emperor responded in strength, and the Nepalese retreated.

The Gurkhas returned three years later, plundering and destroying some famous Tibetan monasteries. The Chinese sent a force of 17,000 which, along with Tibetan troops, drove the Gurkhas out of Tibet and south to within 20 miles of Kathmandu.

Despite this sort of assistance from the Chinese Empire, the people of Tibet chafed under increasingly meddlesome Qing rule.

Between 1804, when the Eighth Dalai Lama died, and 1895, when the Thirteenth Dalai Lama assumed the throne, none of the incumbent incarnations of the Dalai Lama lived to see their nineteenth birthdays.

If the Chinese found a certain incarnation too hard to control, they would poison him. If the Tibetans thought an incarnation was controlled by the Chinese, then they would poison him themselves.

TIBET AND THE GREAT GAME

Throughout this period, Russia and Britain were engaged in the "Great Game," a struggle for influence and control in Central Asia.

Russia pushed south of its borders, seeking access to warm-water sea ports and a buffer zone between Russia proper and the advancing British. The British pushed northward from India, trying to expand their empire and protect the Raj, the "Crown Jewel of the British Empire," from the expansionist Russians.

Tibet was an important playing piece in this game.

Qing Chinese power waned throughout the eighteenth century, as evidenced by its defeat in the Opium Wars with Britain (1839-1842 and 1856-1860), as well as the Taiping Rebellion (1850-1864) and the Boxer Rebellion (1899-1901).

The actual relationship between China and Tibet had been unclear since the early days of the Qing Dynasty, and China's losses at home made the status of Tibet even more uncertain.

The ambiguity of control over Tibet lead to problems. In 1893, the British in India concluded a trade and border treaty with Beijing concerning the boundary between Sikkim and Tibet.

However, the Tibetans flatly rejected the treaty terms.

The British invaded Tibet in 1903 with 10,000 men, and took Lhasa the following year. Thereupon, they concluded another treaty with the Tibetans, as well as Chinese, Nepalese and Bhutanese representatives, which gave the British themselves some control over Tibet's affairs.

THUBTEN GYATSO'S BALANCING ACT

The 13th Dalai Lama, Thubten Gyatso, fled the country in 1904 at the urging of his Russian disciple, Agvan Dorzhiev. He went first to Mongolia, then made his way to Beijing.

The Chinese declared that the Dalai Lama had been deposed as soon as he left Tibet, and claimed full sovereignty over not only Tibet but also Nepal and Bhutan. The Dalai Lama went to Beijing to discuss the situation with the Emperor Guangxu, but he flatly refused to kowtow to the Emperor.

Thubten Gyatso stayed in the Chinese capital from 1906 to 1908.

He returned to Lhasa in 1909, disappointed by Chinese policies towards Tibet. China sent a force of 6,000 troops into Tibet, and the Dalai Lama fled to Darjeeling, India later that same year.

The Chinese Revolution swept away the Qing Dynasty in 1911, and the Tibetans promptly expelled all Chinese troops from Lhasa. The Dalai Lama returned home to Tibet in 1912.

TIBETAN INDEPENDENCE

China's new revolutionary government issued a formal apology to the Dalai Lama for the Qing Dynasty's insults, and offered to reinstate him. Thubten Gyatso refused, stating that he had no interest in the Chinese offer.

He then issued a proclamation that was distributed across Tibet, rejecting Chinese control and stating that "We are a small, religious, and independent nation."

The Dalai Lama took control of Tibet's internal and external governance in 1913, negotiating directly with foreign powers, and reforming Tibet's judicial, penal, and educational systems.

THE SIMLA CONVENTION (1914)

Representatives of Great Britain, China, and Tibet met in 1914 to negotiate a treaty marking out the boundary lines between India and its northern neighbors.

The Simla Convention granted China secular control over "Inner Tibet," (also known as Qinghai Province) while recognizing the autonomy of "Outer Tibet" under the Dalai Lama's rule. Both China and Britain promised to "respect the territorial integrity of [Tibet], and abstain from interference in the administration of Outer Tibet."

China walked out of the conference without signing the treaty after Britain laid claim to the Tawang area of southern Tibet, which is now part of the Indian state of Arunachal Pradesh. Tibet and Britain both signed the treaty.

As a result, China has never agreed to India's rights in northern Arunachal Pradesh (Tawang), and the two nations went to war over the area in 1962. The boundary dispute still has not been resolved.

China also claims sovereignty over all of Tibet, while the Tibetan government-in-exile points to the Chinese failure to sign the Simla Convention as proof that both Inner and Outer Tibet legally remain under the Dalai Lama's jurisdiction.

THE ISSUE RESTS

Soon, China would be too distracted to concern itself with the issue of Tibet.

Japan had invaded Manchuria in 1910, and would advance south and east across large swaths of Chinese territory through 1945.

The new government of the Republic of China would hold nominal power over the majority of Chinese territory for only four years before war broke out between numerous armed factions.

Indeed, the span of Chinese history from 1916 to 1938 came to be called the "Warlord Era," as the different military factions sought to fill the power vacuum left by the collapse of the Qing Dynasty.

China would see near-continuous civil war up to the Communist victory in 1949, and this era of conflict was exacerbated by the Japanese Occupation and World War II. Under such circumstances, the Chinese showed little interest in Tibet.

The 13th Dalai Lama ruled independent Tibet in peace until his death in 1933.

THE 14TH DALAI LAMA

Following Thubten Gyatso's death, the new reincarnation of the Dalai Lama was born in Amdo in 1935.

Tenzin Gyatso, the current Dalai Lama, was taken to Lhasa in 1937 to begin training for his duties as the leader of Tibet. He would remain there until 1959, when the Chinese forced him into exile in India.

PEOPLE'S REPUBLIC OF CHINA INVADES TIBET

In 1950, the People's Liberation Army (PLA) of the newly-formed People's Republic of China invaded Tibet. With stability reestablished in Beijing for the first time in decades, Mao Zedong sought to assert China's right to rule over Tibet as well.

The PLA inflicted a swift and total defeat on Tibet's small army, and China drafted the "Seventeen Point Agreement" incorporating Tibet as an autonomous region of the People's Republic of China.

Representatives of the Dalai Lama's government signed the agreement under protest, and the Tibetans repudiated the agreement nine years later.

COLLECTIVIZATION AND REVOLT

The Mao government of the PRC immediately initiated land redistribution in Tibet.

Landholdings of the monasteries and nobility were seized for redistribution to the peasants. The communist forces hoped to destroy the power base of the wealthy and of Buddhism within Tibetan society.

In reaction, a uprising led by the monks broke out in June of 1956, and continued through 1959. The poorly-armed Tibetans used guerrilla war tactics in an attempt to drive out the Chinese.

The PLA responded by razing entire villages and monasteries to the ground. The Chinese even threatened to blow up the Potala Palace and kill the Dalai Lama, but this threat was not carried out.

Three years of bitter fighting left 86,000 Tibetans dead, according to the Dalai Lama's government in exile.

FLIGHT OF THE DALAI LAMA

On March 1, 1959, the Dalai Lama received an odd invitation to attend a theater performance at PLA headquarters near Lhasa.

The Dalai Lama demurred, and the performance date was postponed until March 10. On March 9, PLA officers notified the Dalai Lama's bodyguards that they would not accompany the Tibetan leader to the performance, nor were they to notify the Tibetan people that he was leaving the palace. (Ordinarily, the people of Lhasa would line the streets to greet the Dalai Lama each time he ventured out.)

The guards immediately publicized this rather ham-handed attempted abduction, and the following day an estimated crowd of 300,000 Tibetans surrounded Potala Palace to protect their leader.

The PLA moved artillery into range of major monasteries and the Dalai Lama's summer palace, Norbulingka.

Both sides began to dig in, although the Tibetan army was much smaller than its adversary, and poorly armed.

Tibetan troops were able to secure a route for the Dalai Lama to escape into India on March 17. Actual fighting began on March 19, and lasted only two days before the Tibetan troops were defeated.

AFTERMATH OF THE 1959 TIBETAN UPRISING

Much of Lhasa lay in ruins on March 20, 1959.

An estimated 800 artillery shells had pummeled Norbulingka, and Lhasa's three largest monasteries were essentially leveled. The Chinese rounded up thousands of monks, executing many of them. Monasteries and temples all over Lhasa were ransacked.

The remaining members of the Dalai Lama's bodyguard were publicly executed by firing squad.

By the time of the 1964 census, 300,000 Tibetans had gone "missing" in the previous five years, either secretly imprisoned, killed, or in exile.

In the days after the 1959 Uprising, the Chinese government revoked most aspects of Tibet's autonomy, and initiated resettlement and land distribution across the country. The Dalai Lama has remained in exile ever since.

China's central government, in a bid to dilute the Tibetan population and provide jobs for Han Chinese, initiated a "Western China Development Program" in 1978.

As many as 300,000 Han now live in Tibet, 2/3 of them in the capital city. The Tibetan population of Lhasa, in contrast, is only 100,000.

Ethnic Chinese hold the vast majority of government posts.

RETURN OF THE PANCHEN LAMA

Beijing allowed the Panchen Lama, Tibetan Buddhism's second-in-command, to return to Tibet in 1989.

He immediately gave a speech before a crowd of 30,000 of the faithful, decrying the harm being done to Tibet under the PRC. He died five days later at the age of 50, allegedly of a massive heart attack.

DEATHS AT DRAPCHI PRISON, 1998

On May 1, 1998, the Chinese officials at Drapchi Prison in Tibet ordered hundreds of prisoners, both criminals and political detainees, to participate in a Chinese flag-raising ceremony.

Some of the prisoners began to shout anti-Chinese and pro-Dalai Lama slogans, and prison guards fired shots into the air before returning all the prisoners to their cells.

The prisoners were then severely beaten with belt buckles, rifle butts, and plastic batons, and some were put into solitary confinement for months at a time, according to one young nun who was released from the prison a year later.

Three days later, the prison administration decided to hold the flag-raising ceremony again.

Once more, some of the prisoners began to shout slogans.

Prison official reacted with even more brutality, and five nuns, three monks, and one male criminal were killed by the guards. One man was shot; the rest were beaten to death.

2008 UPRISING

On March 10, 2008, Tibetans marked the 49th anniversary of the 1959 uprising by peacefully protesting for the release of imprisoned monks and nuns. Chinese police then broke up the protest with tear gas and gunfire.

The protest resumed for several more days, finally turning into a riot. Tibetan anger was fueled by reports that imprisoned monks and nuns were being mistreated or killed in prison as a reaction to the street demonstrations.

Furious Tibetans ransacked and burned the shops of ethnic Chinese immigrants in Lhasa and other cities. The official Chinese media states that 18 people were killed by the rioters.

China immediately cut off access to Tibet for foreign media and tourists.

The unrest spread to neighboring Qinghai (Inner Tibet), Gansu, and Sichuan Provinces. The Chinese government cracked down hard, mobilizing as many as 5,000 troops. Reports indicate that the military killed between 80 and 140 people, and arrested more than 2,300 Tibetans.

The unrest came at a sensitive time for China, which was gearing up for the 2008 Summer Olympics in Beijing.

The situation in Tibet caused increased international scrutiny of Beijing's entire human rights record, leading some foreign leaders to boycott the Olympic Opening Ceremonies. Olympic torch-bearers around the world were met by thousands of human rights protestors.

CONCLUSION

Tibet and China have had a long relationship, fraught with difficulty and change.

At times, the two nations have worked closely together. At other times, they have been at war.

Today, the nation of Tibet does not exist; not one foreign government officially recognizes the Tibetan government-in-exile.

The past teaches us, however, that the geopolitical situation is nothing if not fluid. It is impossible to predict where Tibet and China will stand, relative to one another, one hundred years from now.

Steven Willis

The Chinese View of Tibet Is Dialogue Possible?

During my first trip to China, in the summer of 1978, I was often surprised by how profoundly what the individual sees is influenced by the circle of meaning through which he or she unconsciously interprets events. As a student of rural China and its recent process of collectivization, I was, for instance, enthralled by my first sight of the Chinese countryside. But as our Japanese-made bus wended its way through tiny hamlet after tiny hamlet, what I saw was not the socialist countryside extolled by the Chinese press but immutable China, a China as changeless as the hills in which the villages were nestled. Needing to share my thrill at that first sight, I turned to the young - enthusiastically socialist - Ohio steelworker with whom I happened to be sharing my seat. "I think I could sit like this, looking out the window, watching the peasants and the countryside, for weeks," I exaggerated, by way of opening. "Yes," he agreed, no less excited.

"We're watching millions of Chinese peasants working together to build socialism."

Nowhere could the contrast in pictures be great than when the window frames Tibet and the viewers are the representatives of the Dalai Lama and the Tibetan government-in-exile on the one hand and the government representatives of the People's Republic of China on the other.

For a third party to attempt a new and different version of the truth would be rash indeed, not only because we, too, bring our own images and values to bear but because the facts, in truth, are very difficult to know. What the following pages attempt to do is not to present a new truth about Tibet but rather to present both my understanding of the basic positions and the rationale behind them of the Chinese viewpoint and then to attempt to explain - as much for the Chinese as for ourselves - what about the Chinese position is so often so disquieting to interested Americans.

"Tibet Is an Inalienable Part of China"

The fundamental Chinese position with respect to Tibet is that Tibet is not and never really has been an independent country but has for many centuries been an "inseparable part of multinational China" (PRC

1987). The Chinese turn to history to legitimize their position. The use of history is important because China by both experience and current ideology is profoundly anticolonial and would therefore not wish to be perceived as colonial itself. It is common in China to blame many of its own ills on the effects of Western imperialism, which began with China's defeat at the hands of Britain in the Opium War in 1841 and continued through the Japanese invasion in 1937. Not only does China not recognize the right of governments to acquire territory by conquest but the Chinese Communist Party has long been on record as supporting the rights of nations to self-determination. For the Chinese position to be based on other than historic right would risk the accusation that the Chinese themselves are colonialists. The justice of the Chinese position requires the cooperation of history.

But the historic argument the Chinese make is a difficult one, mixing as it seems to do the apples of China's traditional conception of itself with the oranges of a modern nation-state. Traditionally, the Chinese have viewed themselves as the "Middle Kingdom," the seat of all culture - less a physical, national entity than an idea, a civilization. In the process of expanding the Middle Kingdom, those who had yet to be sinocized were drawn into relations with the Middle Kingdom as vassal states and were expected to pay periodic tribute to the imperial court in recognition of the inferior status of the vassal and the munificence of the rulers of the Middle Kingdom.

The historical arguments adduced by China to support its claim to Tibet derive from a period prior to best, may have been a vassal of the Middle Kingdom. The Chinese view of that history, quite naturally, is an ethnocentric one that denies Tibet its own independent, complex, rich and idiosyncratic history. Admittedly, many of the basic facts of that history. Admittedly, many of the basic facts of that history as the Chinese tell it would be recognizable to both sides. How the Chinese tell the tale, however, is where the historical difference lies. The history of Chinese-Tibetan relations is covered in more detail in van Walt's article (this issue), but a few examples of the difference in telling will help understanding here.

The Chinese history, as it is currently and officially proclaimed, begins with the marriage, in 641 A.D. during the Tang dynasty, of Chinese Princess Wen Cheng to the then ruler of a newly unified Tibet, Songzain Gambo. One of her presents to her husband and the people of Tibet was the huge statue of Sakyamuni, still enshrined in Lhasa's Jokhang Cathedral, Tibet's most sacred shrine. Thus, Princess When Cheng, and therefore China, is credited with having introduced

Buddhism into Tibet. Their marital alliance is seen as the first step in the later incorporation of Tibet into the Middle Kingdom.

But from the Tibetan perspective, Songzain Gambo is to their country what Qin Shi Huangdi is to China - the unifier and founding father, the codifier and introducer (from India) of a Tibetan script, the initiator of written history. The Tibetan history would note that Songzain Gambo married not only China's Princes Wen Cheng but Nepal's Princess Bhrikuti, whose role in the introduction of Buddhism to Tibet is considered no less important than that of the Chinese princess. More importantly, Princess Wen Cheng was given in marriage most reluctantly and under threat of force. The Chinese at the time recognized the Kingdom of Tibet as a "Strong, independent, and expansionist power...a serious rival to China in Central Asia". The marriage, in short, was a political balance of power act by Songzain Gambo, an expression of Tibetan independence and a victory for Tibet rather than China.

The Chinese interpretation of the China-Tibet treaty of 821, the text of which still stands inscribed in stone in front of the Jokhang, reveals a similar ethnocentricity, emphasizing the "uncle-nephew" nature of the alliance and therefore China's superiority. It ignores that part of the treaty that states that both Tibet and China shall keep the country and frontiers of which they now are in possession. The whole region to the east of that being the country of Great China and the whole region to the west being assuredly the country of Great Tibet, from either side of that frontier there shall be no warfare, no hostile invasions, and no seizure of territory.

Similarly, the actual "incorporation" of Tibet into China is strangely attributed to Genghis Khan and his later successor, Kublai Khan. Strangely, because Genghis Khan and Kublai Khan were not Chinese but Mongolian, and the dynasty they established - the Yuan - incorporated not only China but, for a brief period, the largest empire the world has ever seen. Moreover, the Mongolian Khans turned for their legitimacy not to the Chinese past but to the Buddhist universal emperors of Tibet and India.

To be sure, the cho-yon relationship, whereby the Mongolian prince protected the Tibetan lama and his teachings in return for the lama's ministering to the religious needs of the Mongolian patron, began during this period and would later become the basis of the relationship between Tibet and China under the Manchu dynasty. But the fundamental relationship of Tibet during the Yuan dynasty, and for centuries thereafter, was with the Mongols rather than the Chinese, and the nature of the relationship was not incorporation but military protection in return for spiritual autonomy. Out of this relationship grew the institution of the Dalai Lama; a Mongolian Khan first conferred the title of Tala (Dalai).

It was really only during the Manchu dynasty, and particularly during the reign of Kang Xi, that Tibetan-Chinese relations developed to the point that the independence of Tibet became an issue of abiding ambiguity. The Qing dynasty saw the beginning of the power struggles between Great Britain, Russia and China for dominance in Central Asia. Tibet turned for protection to China, sacrificing - at the height of Manchu power - the right to an independent foreign policy while maintaining de facto control over internal, domestic Tibetan affairs.

Tibet's perspective on these events never abrogates its conception of itself as an independent state; China's view increasingly argues otherwise. Indeed, although the basis for the argument has differed, with Chiang Kaishek asserting that Tibetans were part of a single Chinese race and the Communists recognizing them as a "national minority," both the Nationalists of Chiang and the Communists of Mao Zedong have agreed that Tibet is an inalienable and inseparable part of China.

"Chinese Rule Has Been Good"

A second fundamental position of the Chinese today is that Communist rule in Tibet, whatever mistakes may have been made, has been good for Tibet and far better than rule under the Dalai Lama. The argument relies on a felicitous blend of the ideology of Marxist-Leninist Mao Zedong Thought on the one hand and traditional Chinese prejudices toward the Tibetan people on the other. In placing Tibet with the Marxist stages of historical development that trace from primitive communal society, to slave society, to feudalism, capitalism, socialism and ultimately to communism, the Chinese determined that Tibet at the time of the Communist takeover in 1950 was a theocratic, feudal serfdom, therefore considerably more backward than Han China proper. Moreover, it was regarded as a particularly "cruel and barbaric" system with the three estate holders (the nobility, monasteries and the officials), who accounted for less than 5 percent of the population, owning all of Tibet's cultivated land and subjecting the vast majority of the population - the serfs - quite literally to slavery. The evils wrought by this oppressive system have formed the subject of many a Chinese movie and photo exhibit (usually in the Minorities Cultural Palace in Beijing), convincing even the most educated Chinese of the Tibetans' barbarity by presenting evidence of the mutilations that were a regular form of punishment in Tibet - the gouged-out eyes and hacked-off noses and hands, the bones of murdered slaves that the monks carved into flutes, the scorpion pit where criminals were slowly eaten alive by deadly insects, the human skin used to make drums and the bizarre and unsavory sexual practices of the Tibetan people in which one wife serves several brothers.

Thus, although the Communists initially agreed (on paper, at least) to grant substantial autonomy to Tibet and to neither challenge the status of the Dalai Lama nor interfere in the area's religious practices, the Communists, no doubt quite genuinely, saw their takeover as a "liberation" of the Tibetan people (though it is more difficult to understand why, given the fighting in the far eastern part of Tibet, that liberation is also described as "peaceful") and assumed that the Tibetans themselves would soon come to share that point of view as well. Such resistance as continued may have puzzled the Chinese but could easily be interpreted as the efforts of a small handful of the Tibetan feudal ruling class who had not resigned themselves to the reforms that the new, "democratic" era would bring.

Although the "democratic" reforms that began after the departure of the Dalai Lama in 1959 brought Tibet one step further in the Marxian progression toward socialism and ultimately to communism, Tibet remains in Chinese eyes more backward than Han China proper and, therefore, in need of fraternal help. The Chinese are fond of statistics, and the array that have been gathered to support the extent of aid given and therefore of progress made in Tibet is impressive, however difficult such statistics may be to evaluate. State subsidies (10,000 yuan between 1952 and 1986), capital construction (40 new projects since 1984), goods (378 million yuan worth sent since 1983), roads (21,500 km of highways) and schools (three institutions of higher learning, 14 secondary technical schools, 64 middle schools, 3,280 primary schools) are but a few of the benefits said to have come to Tibet in recent years.

The government does admit to "mistakes" with respect to its handling of Tibet, particularly during the Cultural Revolution, when" 'leftist' thinking disrupted production and construction, the people's living standards did not improve, and many monasteries were damaged or destroyed." But the government points out that the problems of the Cultural Revolution were not peculiar to Tibet but were nationwide in impact and that the leftist influences have been eliminated and the policy of free religious belief has been "better" implemented.

The most sophisticated Chinese - those not speaking publicly in official capacities - would note the irony of Americans who, in supporting the Dalai Lama and therefore an independent Tibet, seem also to be supporting a social and political system (a theocratic state) both greatly at odds with our own ethical and political values and so demonstrably inferior to the system introduced by the Chinese. Indeed, however unseemly and unsettling the Chinese use of worst-case examples to buttress their propaganda on Tibet, there is sufficient evidence from the few Westerners who visited pre-1949 Tibet of widespread corruption among lamas and cruelly primitive forms of punishment that few (the Dalai Lama included) would want to argue for a return to the old system.

But the substitution of one form of oppression for another can hardly be considered progress; to oppose the second form does not necessarily represent a call for a return to the first. The evidence from Tibetan refugees and from recent travelers in Tibet (detailed elsewhere in this issue) of massive Chinese abuse of human rights and widespread death through execution, neglect and abuse of prisoners and starvation; of wholesale destruction of the nation's monasteries and assault on its religious traditions; and of the gross misuse of power by Han Chinese cadres is over-whelming. Outsiders who know of such abuse and remain silent are morally irresponsible.

"Interference in China's Internal Affairs Is Unacceptable"

The third Chinese position with respect to Tibet is that public disagreement with the Chinese position, particularly with respect to the question of independence, represents to the question of independence, represents interference in the internal affairs of China and hence is unacceptable. Thus, the Dalai Lama is seen as leading a very small "separatist clique," representative not of the Tibetan people as a whole but of the illegitimate 5 percent of the aristocratic upper classes.

The goal of the Dalai Lama and his separatist clique is to "stage a comeback," to restore the cruel and barbaric serf system that prevailed until his departure in 1959, at which time the people of Tibet were unexpectedly liberated sooner than originally planned. On the record, the Chinese oppose the Dalai Lama's political activities in other countries and any of his statements that are detrimental to the unification of the motherland and unity among all its nationalities. The Chinese government also opposes meetings between the Dalai Lama or his representatives and officials of any other country.

Indications of support for the Dalai Lama by the US Congress or any of its members are also therefore seen as interfering in China's internal affairs - as "unbridled actions," "sinister slander" and serious incidents "engineered by a small number of people." The continuation of such support is said to threaten the friendly relations between China and the US and to "hurt the feelings of the Chinese people."

Is Dialogue Possible?

Given the dramatically different ways in which Chinese, Tibetans and interested Americans view Tibet, is there any room for dialogue? Can the issues be reformulated so they are easier to discuss? Given a certain degree of willingness on both sides, and with time and patience, the answer may be yes. Several delegations representing the Dalai Lama have visited Tibet in recent years, and however disgruntled the Chinese may have been with their ensuing reports, the willingness to receive such delegations is an important opportunity for dialogue. Several concessions would be useful for furthering that dialogue.

First, it would help merely for the Chinese to acknowledges that distinctive cultures and histories result in distinctively different points of view. It is simply not true, as the Chinese claim, that "Every honest foreigner who has been to Tibet can see that the Tibetan people are enjoying religious freedom and democracy." To the contrary, many honest foreigners see a land ravaged by the destruction of its religious edifices, one in which Tibetans are often dominated by condescending Chinese.

Second, the issue of Tibetan independence needs to be recast. The historical argument that Tibet has "always been an inalienable part of Chinese territory" is unconvincing. Tibet has maintained a unique, autonomous and distinctive culture, religion and political system for centuries. But it is also true that Tibet is completely idiosyncratic, that it never became a nation-state in the modern sense of the word. The Chinese properly recognize and stress that Tibet has never been recognized by other nations as in independent nation. (Nor, given history since 1950, is this likely to happen now.)

The US government's position, that Tibet is a part of China, is not based on history. Rather, it is a position that is simply self-consciously stated without further articulation. If the question of Tibetan independence were recast in terms of the necessity of granting genuine autonomy to Tibet - autonomy that respects the uniqueness of Tibet's history, culture and religion and permits the Tibetan people to develop along lines that they themselves freely choose - considerable room is left for both sides to negotiate the precise details of constructing that autonomy without undue threat to China.

The Chinese may argue that they have already granted autonomy to Tibet, that Tibet, after all, is an "autonomous region." But the promise of China to maintain "one country, two systems" in Hong Kong and

Taiwan and the need to convince both places - but Taiwan in particular - that they will be allowed to maintain their distinctive systems, would gain substantial credence were major concessions made in Tibet.

Third, the Chinese must understand not only that the Western belief in human rights is deeply held but those beliefs transcend government - both our own and others. Similarly, they must understand the very high regard with which the leading international human rights organizations are held - not just in the US but in the West in general. To raise the issues of other governments but rather to act on behalf of our common humanity, regardless of government. Only years after the Cultural Revolution has the full extent of its turmoil, destruction and violence come to be understood in the West.

Few would be willing to make the same mistake again by not believing the stories of refugees from Tibet. Scholars of China made a terrible mistake during the Cultural Revolution. Many did not believe or did not give proper credence to the stories of violence and world disintegration being told by the refugees who had risked their lives to flee to Hong Kong. So long as those stories continue to tell of human rights abuse in Tibet, the international human rights abuse in Tibet, the international human rights organization will continue to bring those abuses to the attention of the world public and to demand redress from the Chinese government. Chinese claims to have ended those abuses and their assertions that there are no (or only 27) political prisoners in Tibet would be greatly enhanced by cooperating with such international human rights groups and inviting them to learn more about recent reforms in Tibet.

Fourth, the Chinese must how profoundly different their picture of the Dalai Lama is from that American public. The Dalai Lama is viewed in the West as the quintessential man of peace. The Chinese separatist clique that seeks to restore the self-system to Tibet is at glaring odds with the image the Dalai Lama himself projects. The contrast between the man who claims "my message is always the same: to cultivate and practice love, kindness, compassion and tolerance" with those who claim the Dalia Lama is "Openly" trumpeting for the independence of Tibet" and "splitting the motherland, sabotaging the national unity and jeopardizing the interests of the people of the Tibetan nationality" is not designed to win much support for the Chinese side.

However bad the organization of Tibetan life may have been prior to 1949, the Dalai Lama himself has always been revered, and he has introduced major democratic reforms into the refugee population at Dharamsala.

The Chinese have said that they are willing to "forgive" the Dalai Lama and let bygones by bygones, forgetting what happened with the uprising and his escape in 1959. The Dalai Lama, so long as he is willing to "safeguard the unification of the motherland," is welcome to return to China, neither living nor holding political position in Tibet but residing rather in Beijing and holding the posts of vice-chairman of both the Standing Committee of the National People's Congress and the Chinese People's Political Consultative Congress. The Chinese will have to go well beyond that position, but that at least is a start.

A resolution of these issues would require concessions on the part of the Tibetan side as well, and ample evidence exists of a willingness to make them. In recent years, as China has emerged from its decades of isolation and hostility to the West and has joined the international system, it, too, has been willing to make major concessions on a wide variety of important issues. The campaign against "spiritual pollution" from the West in 1983 came to a rapid halt when Western businesses expressed their concern about future investment in so unpredictable and potentially unstable a policy.

Recriminations against student demonstrators early last year may have been milder because of a watchful and openly concerned Western public. No longer does the Chinese government speak of "liberating" Taiwan but rather of "reunification" with Taiwan; the formula of "one country, two systems" for Hong Kong is a major change of view. Our different values and historical pasts mean that we will forever look out the same window and see very different scenes. But by discussing our values and our views with a minimum of recrimination, keeping the variety of channels of communication open, we at least stand a chance that the differences are in the shades and the hues rather than in the very picture itself.

www.ingramcontent.com/pod-product-compliance
Lightning Source LLC
Chambersburg PA
CBHW021058080526
44587CB00010B/295